U

MODERN SPIRITUAL MASTERS
Robert Ellsberg, Series Editor

This series introduces the writing and vision of some of the great spiritual masters of the twentieth century. Along with selections from their writings, each volume includes a comprehensive introduction, presenting the author's life and writings in context and drawing attention to points of special relevance to contemporary spirituality.

Some of these authors found a wide audience in their lifetimes. In other cases recognition has come long after their deaths. Some are rooted in long-established traditions of spirituality. Others charted new, untested paths. In each case, however, the authors in this series have engaged in a spiritual journey shaped by the influences and concerns of our age. Such concerns include the challenges of modern science, religious pluralism, secularism, and the quest for social justice.

At the dawn of a new millennium this series commends these modern spiritual masters, along with the saints and witnesses of previous centuries, as guides and companions to a new generation of seekers.

EVELYN UNDERHILL

Essential Writings

Selected
with an Introduction by
EMILIE GRIFFIN

ORBIS BOOKS

Maryknoll, New York 10545

Founded in 1970, Orbis Books endeavors to publish works that enlighten the mind, nourish the spirit, and challenge the conscience. The publishing arm of the Maryknoll Fathers and Brothers, Orbis seeks to explore the global dimensions of the Christian faith and mission, to invite dialogue with diverse cultures and religious traditions, and to serve the cause of reconciliation and peace. The books published reflect the views of their authors and do not represent the official position of the Maryknoll Society. To learn more about Maryknoll and Orbis Books, please visit our website at www.maryknoll.org.

Library of Congress Cataloging-in-Publication Data
Underhill, Evelyn, 1875-1941.
  [Selections. 2003]
  Evelyn Underhill : essential writings / selected with an introduction by Emilie Griffin.
    p. cm. – (Modern spiritual masters series)
  ISBN 1-57075-471-3 (pbk.)
  1. Mysticism. 2. Spiritual life – Anglican Communion. I. Griffin, Emilie. II. Title. III. Series.
  BV5082.3 .U53 2003
  248.2'2 – dc21

                                                        2002015367

Contents

Introduction

The Practical Mystic

Evelyn Underhill (1875–1941) is one of the most widely read writers on Christian spirituality, especially on mysticism. Today's keen interest in the mystical life may be traced in great part to her influence.

In 1911 Underhill seemed to burst out of nowhere onto the London intellectual scene with the publication of *Mysticism: A Study in the Nature and Development of Man's Spiritual Consciousness*. At the time mysticism was suspect in both intellectual and religious circles. The writings of the great mystics were nearly lost, and certainly out of print. Underhill helped not only to revive the tradition, but also to restore respect for mysticism as a normal — rather than paranormal — dimension of religious experience.

Underhill was thirty-six when *Mysticism* appeared. Until then she had been a writer of light verse and fanciful novels. *Mysticism*, however, could not be slighted or ignored. Intellectuals were impressed. Among them was the formidable Baron Friedrich von Hügel, who became her friend, colleague, and mentor.

A wider reading public was also attracted by Underhill's ideas. In subsequent works she spoke to believers and unbelievers alike with high seriousness and flashes of humor. For the preparation of the mystic, she insisted, hard work and discipline would be needed: "if not the renunciation of the cloister, then at least the virtues of the golf course." With her readers she adopted a strong magisterial tone: "Yet it is to you, practical man, reading these pages as you rush through the tube...that this message so needed by your time — or rather, your want of time, — is addressed."[1] Mystical consciousness could not be confined to the cloister or the hermitage, and to underscore the point, she drew much of her imagery from the street scenes of London: "Look with the eye of contemplation upon the most dissipated tabby of the streets, and you shall discern the celestial quality of life set like an aureole about his tattered ears."[2] When this bedraggled tabby ran up a "sooty tree" the tree also invited contemplation: "It contains for you the whole divine cycle of the seasons; upon the plane of quiet, its inward pulse is clearly to be heard." The reader must gaze, must look with intensity, "as you would look into the eyes of a friend, selflessly, ardently."[3] And soon the reader would begin to experience the rewards of contemplative living. Underhill made spiritual life a vivid possibility. The high reaches of prayer could belong to — well, not everybody — but to anyone willing to apply the spiritual disciplines. Over a lifetime of offering this message, and living it, in various ways, Underhill made an impact. She led retreats, offered spiritual direction, wrote thirty books and more than four hundred articles. For men and women who saw themselves as ordinary Christians, Underhill opened new doors to spiritual life.

It was odd, really, because Evelyn Underhill had grown up in a rather agnostic family. Of course, the Underhills were Church of England, and went through the respectable motions. But religious zeal, or even belief, was hardly the family's style.

Something about her family life did, however, encourage her to excel. Raised in London, she was the only child of Arthur Underhill, a barrister, and his wife, Alice Lucy Ironmonger. Arthur, who had studied metaphysics and philosophy at Trinity College, Dublin, certainly encouraged his daughter's prodigious curiosity. He also taught her to sail. In 1888, when Evelyn was thirteen, she took a cruise with her father on his yacht, *The Amoretta*, and kept the ship's log for the month-long journey. Another influence was formative in her first twelve years: a friendship with two brothers, Jeff and Hubert, of the neighboring Stuart Moore family. Jeff was slightly younger than she, Hubert somewhat older. Both boys were keen on sailing, as Evelyn was. Both were planning to follow their father into law careers.

Wit and intelligence are evident in her letters home from Sandgate House, a boarding school: "Oh! please can you tell me who Spinoza was, he was mentioned in the sermon last Sunday; he seems to have been a not very nice person from what Mr. Wakefield said." Such frisky high spirits and robust intellect are matched by an early interest in spiritual discipline. Underhill at this period was a romantic: "In real life I most admire Mahomet, because he was sincere, Giordano Bruno, because he was strong for the truth, and Jesus Christ, because ethically he was perfect, and always thought of the weak ones first."[4] In her last year at Sandgate House, 1891, she was confirmed in the Church of England at Christ Church, Folkestone, and made her First Communion on Easter Sunday. After leaving school she attended King's College for Women in London, where she studied history and botany.[5]

Like many of her era, Underhill wandered far in search of God. Her interest in the supernatural, even the preternatural, in paranormal phenomena, led her to examine many forms of spiritual life outside of the Christian fold. In doing so she was influenced by the fashionable thought-currents of her time. Christopher Armstrong, in his account of her life, speaks of the social and cultural milieu of the Edwardian era as "mysteriously compounded of the psychic, the psychological, the occult, the mystical, the medieval, the advance of science, the self-unfolding of the Absolute, the apotheosis of Art, the re-discovery of the feminine and an infatuation with both the unashamedly sensuous and the most ethereally 'spiritual.'" Under these influences the young Underhill fled from the staid and respectable Anglicanism in which she had been raised. Among her friends and associates were Arthur Machen and Arthur Waite, who influenced her toward membership (probably about 1905) in The Hermetic Society of the Golden Dawn. How seriously did they take it? It is hard to say.

But Armstrong suggests that the Golden Dawn (informally referred to as G.D.) permitted them "the acquisition of a certain
'gnosis' or private experiential contact with ultimate realities"
through the performance of certain rituals.[6] One of the writers
who affected her at the same period was Maurice Maeterlinck
(also an influence on C. S. Lewis and many others), who "had a
mystic turn of mind."[7]

"For eight or nine years I really believed myself to be an athe-
ist," Underhill wrote. Apparently these years were after she left
school and during her early twenties. "Philosophy brought me
round to an intelligent and responsible sort of theism which I enjoyed thoroughly but which did not last long. Gradually the net
closed in on me and I was driven nearer and nearer to Christianity, half of me wishing it were true and the other half resisting
violently all the time."[8]

During these same years of pondering religion and philosophy, Evelyn first gravitated to the writing of poetry and fiction.
A Bar-Lamb's Ballad Book, a collection of light verse about
the legal profession, appeared in 1902. (Both her father and
her close friend, Hubert Stuart Moore, were barristers.) She
wrote three published novels: *The Grey World* (1904), *The Lost
Word* (1907), and *The Column of Dust* (1908). These works,
and her short stories of this period, focused on spiritual questions, with varying degrees of success as fiction. The hero of *The
Grey World,* Willie Hopkinson, gives up the world of ordinary
and commonplace experience to go in search of solitude and
perfection. In *The Lost Word,* an architect, Paul Valery, is the
protagonist who moves in the opposite direction. Valery, who has
been consumed by the single aspiration of building a magnificent
church, fails to do so, and accepts a more ordinary, fleshly existence instead. In these early works Underhill is struggling with
her own understanding of matter and spirit, wrestling with the
need to live in both eternal and finite worlds.[9] In the years that
followed she continued to write and publish some verse, but her
interest in fiction did not continue.

By late 1906 Evelyn was showing a marked interest in things Roman Catholic. Her friends thought she might soon "go over to Rome." In 1907 she made a retreat with her friend Ethel Ross Barker at the Franciscan Convent of St. Mary of the Angels, at Southampton. There she was (in her own phrase) "converted" and said, "an overwhelming vision convinced me that the Catholic religion is true." In spite of that, Underhill refrained from becoming a Roman Catholic. She felt ambivalent, in part because of the papal encyclical *Pascendi* (issued September 1907).[10] The encyclical condemned Modernism, an intellectual movement to which Underhill felt sympathy. There was also her engagement to consider. She had been engaged for a year to her childhood friend Hubert Stuart Moore. Efforts to reconcile her fiancé to Roman Catholicism were unsuccessful. He feared that the Roman Catholic practice of confession would introduce a third party into the marriage. Evelyn had her own uncertainties about Catholic allegiance. Without question, there was still a strong prejudice against Catholics among people of her station, Catholicism being regarded as a religion of the illiterate and uneducated. But Underhill refrained from becoming Catholic principally because of her fiancé's objection. She married Hubert Stuart Moore on July 3, 1907. Mass was said for them on their wedding day by their friend Robert Hugh Benson, a Catholic priest. Benson, also a writer, was well known as a priest-convert from Anglicanism.

After her marriage she continued to attend Roman Catholic masses from time to time without receiving the sacrament. Her studies in the spiritual life intensified as she concentrated her efforts on *Mysticism*.

After *Mysticism* was published, Underhill came to know Baron Friedrich von Hügel (1852–1925), the major Roman Catholic scholar living in England. Generally admiring the book, the baron also offered to give her an extensive critique.[11] A friend of Ernst Troeltsch and Cuthbert Butler, as well as a correspondent of William James, von Hügel was counted among the most learned men of his time. His two-volume study, *The Mystical Element of*

Religion as Studied in Saint Catherine of Genoa and her Friends,
first published in 1908 and reprinted with a new introduction in
1923, was thought to be a masterpiece. Long and cumbersome
in style, the work mingled a philosophy of religion, a historical
account of Catherine of Genoa, and theological interpretations.
This study, thirty years in the making, seven in the writing, had
put von Hügel at the pinnacle in the study of religion.[12] In Underhill he found a kindred spirit, more than twenty years younger,
but with an intelligence equally able to plumb the subject matter. He supported her work but did not always approve; he gave
pointed comments and critiques on her ideas.

Von Hügel's concerns were, among others, that Underhill's
mystics were not thoroughly grounded in the real world. He also
thought that Underhill had failed to keep the difference between
God and the soul sufficiently clear. He called to her attention,
as Dana Greene puts it, "the book's particularly anti-historical,
anti-institutional, and monistic biases."[13] Other Catholic scholars, among them John Chapman, the future abbot of Downside,
voiced similar complaints. After a thorough reading, von Hügel
sent Underhill a number of "corrections," which she reflected
in later editions. But she did not compromise her original vision and especially resisted his suggestion that she "re-think"
the work.[14] Whatever the criticism, Underhill's achievement was
widely admired. Among the favorable comments and reviews,
Underhill herself mentions two: a review in *The Record,* "most
generous in its language...great book, classic work, etc. and a
long and splendid review signed C. E. Laurence from *The Daily
Graphic.*"[15]

Underhill's achievement as a significant writer on mysticism
has held up well over time. In his 1984 study, *Christian Mysticism: The Future of a Tradition,* Harvey Egan acknowledges
Underhill's influence. He admires her statement that "mysticism
is no isolated vision, no fugitive glimpse of reality, but a complete
system of life carrying its own guarantees and obligations....It is
the name of that organic process which involves the perfect consummation of the Love of God: the achievement here and now of

the immortal heritage of man.... It is an ordered movement towards ever higher levels of reality, ever closer identification with the Infinite."[16] In citing these texts, Egan praises the wholeness of Underhill's vision. According to him, she proposes the mystical way as a "complete system of life," a way of living. Egan admires her because "she stands as a strong counterpoint to the contemporary tendency to reduce mysticism to transient experiences, especially moments of ecstatic rapture. She resolutely refuses to identify the mystical as the ecstatic."[17]

Underhill puts secondary mystical phenomena, such as visions, locutions, ecstasies, and raptures, in a larger context. These phenomena may or may not occur; but they are not crucial to the mystical life, which is an "ordered movement," an awakening of the self to God, by which the self is purified, illuminated, and finally united to God. Underhill clears away the underbrush of magical or paranormal occurrences. The Christian mystic focuses entirely on the one God.

Underhill also singles out five other characteristics of authentic mysticism. First, it is active and practical, requiring attention and pursuit of its Object. Such comparisons as "quest" or "pilgrimage" convey this sense of pursuit. Second, mysticism is entirely spiritual and transcendental, having no interest in magical control over worldly events. Rather than tapping into spiritual forces, the mystic wants to let go and surrender all to God. The true mystic by his or her focus on God redirects everything else and places it in a subordinate or secondary status. Third, mysticism is centered in love: "the business and method of mysticism is love."[18] God is experienced as the Beloved, no impersonal Absolute. Fourth, union with God in authentic mysticism transforms the self for ever richer levels of life. Fifth, the authentic mystic, because of this loving union, becomes unselfish. The mystic is not seeking his or her own happiness, virtue, or well-being, though by surrendering self such blessings are often heaped upon him or her. The true mystic is not looking for peak experiences or altered states of consciousness. No, the genuine mystic is on a course of radical self-forgetting, self-surrendering, and self-transcending. Thus

Underhill distinguishes the authentic mystic from those who are looking for a spiritual high.

Bernard McGinn, another contemporary scholar of mysticism, is more reserved in his praise. He insists that Underhill be taken seriously as a scholar in spite of her popular style. However, he also notes that she adopts two positions that have been questioned in recent years. She identifies mysticism with the core of religion and she argues for transcultural and transreligious unity to the stages of the mystic path. Nevertheless, McGinn regards her as a substantial thinker and writer on mysticism.[19]

Underhill's *Mysticism* was not merely a work of spiritual enthusiasm. Her book provided a critical examination of the psychological aspects of mystical prayer. She recovered for her readers some important mystics who had been neglected or forgotten. In addition to Teresa of Avila and St. John of the Cross she mentions Jacopone da Todi, Mechthild of Magdeburg, Angela of Foligno, Jacob Boehme, Brother Lawrence, and others of still greater obscurity. Ranging easily through centuries, Underhill combined such obscure references with familiar snatches from many well-known British poets, like Henry Vaughan, William Blake, Robert Browning, and Alfred, Lord Tennyson. She explained "the life-process of the mystic," including stages in the mystical journey, and pointed to a higher synthesis which she called "the crown of human evolution."[20]

Underhill continued to write shorter and more accessible works on the mystical life. In these, her focus shifted. *The Path of Eternal Wisdom: A Mystical Commentary on the Way of the Cross* (1911) and *The Spiral Way: Being Fifteen Meditations on the Soul's Ascent* (1912) were both published under the pseudonym John Cordelier. (A cordelier is a Franciscan of the Strict Observance who wears a cincture of knotted cord.) Each volume took a religious viewpoint and offered meditations on events in the life of Jesus Christ. She was also writing commentaries (in her own name) on "The Cloud of Unknowing" (*The Seeker* 6, no. 24 [February 1911]) and the "Mirror of Simple Souls" (*The Fortnightly Review* 78 [February

1911]). Later on that year *The Seeker* ran Underhill's "The Message of Ruysbroeck" in two parts.

In 1913 her book *The Mystic Way: A Psychological Study in Christian Origins* appeared. Using Christian materials, Underhill returned to the scholar's voice, offering study and interpretation rather than spiritual instruction. The two moods would remain throughout her writing career.

Between 1914 and 1918, when England was at war, Underhill worked on the Naval Intelligence (Africa) guidebooks. She also wrote and published such popular volumes as *The Path of Eternal Wisdom* (1911), *The Spiral Way* (1912), and *Practical Mysticism* (1914). *Essentials of Mysticism* appeared in 1920.

The philosopher Henri Bergson, well known for his doctrine of the *Élan Vital,* or "life force," and specializing in intuitive consciousness, became one of her heroes. Bergson held that God works in the processes of evolution and that the "life force" is a form of divine expression. Evelyn Underhill heard Bergson lecture in London in 1912. She celebrated him in an article, "Bergson and the Mystics." Bergson, she claimed, was the link between the mystics and "the inarticulate explorers of the infinite."[21]

Late in 1912, Underhill became aware of the Indian mystic Rabindranath Tagore, who was all the rage in London. She reviewed three of his books in *The Nation*. The following year, 1913, Tagore received the Nobel Prize for Literature. Throughout 1913 Underhill worked directly with Tagore to prepare a translation of a hundred poems attributed (as it happens, incorrectly) to Kabir, a fifteenth-century Bengali mystical poet. Also Underhill worked on an introduction to an autobiography of Tagore's father, Maharishi Devendranath Tagore.

Underhill had a high opinion of Rabindranath Tagore. After coming to know him well she still called him a "master." What attracted her was the positive character of his mystical vision, because (she stated) "it accepts life in its wholeness as a revelation of the Divine mind."[22]

"Mysticism is the art of union with reality," Underhill wrote in *Practical Mysticism*. Subtitling the work *A Little Book for*

Normal People, she meant to address both the serious inquirer and the idly curious. In this work she made observations that can best be called tongue-in-cheek. If her readers had been bewildered by the loose talk of mysticism running wild at London dinner parties, she meant to set them straight. Mildly condescending to those who would not read the mystics for themselves, or who pretended that if they did they could not understand them, Underhill flashed a certain scholarly edge. Her aim was to demystify the mystics; she believed they could be understood by virtually everyone.

In 1921 she gave the Upton Lectures on Religion, Manchester College, Oxford. It was the first time that such an invitation had been extended to a woman. These lectures were soon published under the title *The Life of the Spirit and the Life of Today.* No doubt she was a formidable visitor among the college dons. Of one such encounter, at King's College, Cambridge, she wrote: "I sat at the theology table, between X. and Y., and managed to be polite while they talked of 'superstition.' But oh, how these intellectualists miss the bus!"[23]

Also in 1921 Underhill took steps to resolve the issues that had long kept her from active church membership. She approached her longtime friend Baron von Hügel to become her spiritual director. Under his guidance Underhill returned to active membership in the Church of England.

Some have supposed that von Hügel cautioned Underhill against becoming a Roman Catholic because of the obvious concerns about loss of intellectual freedom. But this is not at all certain. The baron, himself an ardent, if critical, Catholic, would have been glad to see her become Roman Catholic, if he had felt the Spirit moving her in that direction. Yet he was also conscious of the explicit demands of obedience being made upon Catholic intellectuals in his day.[24] As a scholar who knew many of the important Catholic thinkers of his own time, von Hügel had narrowly escaped being condemned as a Modernist. Two others of his close acquaintance, the biblical scholar Alfred Loisy and the Jesuit George Tyrrell, had been condemned. Tyrrell had been expelled from the Jesuits for his opposition to ecclesiastical authority in biblical interpretation; he was also excommunicated. This controversy was at its height in the first two decades of the twentieth century.

The Modernists espoused many of the most attractive religious ideas of the period, ideas which were not exclusive to Modernism, many of which would afterwards prevail. Among their best ideas were: faith as a personal encounter; appreciation of religious experience and spiritual anthropology; deeper probing of the relationship between psychology and religion, a return to the traditional emphasis on a sense of mystery; growth in insight in the development of dogma; affirmation of the organic nature of the church and the importance of the laity; and a call to leave a cultural ghetto. These were not Modernist, but modern ideas. They were "the wave of the future" in von Hügel's and Underhill's time.

In any event, after years of hovering at the edge of Roman Catholicism, Underhill at last became a full participant in Anglican sacramental life and worship; she began to lead retreats and give lectures in many settings.

Another documented aspect of von Hügel's direction is that he encouraged Underhill to focus on a relationship with Jesus Christ. Recounting this experience later on, she stated that before her encounter with von Hügel as director she had not had any personal experience of the Lord. Gently but firmly, von Hügel had insisted that being "theocentric" was not enough. Within four months Underhill reported that a direct relationship with Jesus began to develop. She attributed this to von Hügel's instruction and his prayers.[25]

Still another important facet of the baron's influence is that he encouraged Underhill to "de-intellectualize" her religion. In particular he instructed her to visit the poor twice a week. He counseled her about the amounts of time spent in prayer, about particular friendships and detachment, about time spent in directing others. Though he sounds (in his letters) rather stern at times, it is clear that they had a comfortable relationship.

Von Hügel counseled her during times of intense scrupulos-
ity. Their exchanges were often intense and even heated. As we
might put it, Underhill was hard on herself. She doubted the truth
of her experience of God; she wondered if she had been subject
to self-deceit or self-delusion. In all such crises, von Hügel offered steady, fatherly reassurance. He assured her that God, in
Christ, comes down to us and crosses the uncrossable distance so
that we, in cheerful confidence, can go about the business of our
daily lives.

After von Hügel's death in 1925, Underhill continued in spiritual direction with two important Anglicans, Walter Howard
Frere, bishop of Truro, and Reginald Somerset Ward. That year
also marked the publication of her last big work on mysticism,
The Mystics of the Church, which expressly located the mystics, ancient and modern, firmly within the Christian churches.
Man and the Supernatural followed in 1927, a last tribute to
von Hügel's influence, in which she tried to capture what he had
taught her.

Underhill was much in demand as a retreat leader throughout the 1920s and early 1930s. From 1926 to 1934 she gave
seven or eight retreats each year, both to lay people and clergy,
in such spiritual centers as Pleshey, Moreton, Leiston Abbey,
Glastonbury, Little Compton, Water Millock, St. Leonard's, and
St. Michael's Home. Of one of her talks at Pleshey, Lucy Menzies
wrote: "When the actual retreat was about to begin, I remember
the expectancy in the chapel as her quiet voice broke its stillness. And it was all so natural, nothing forced or 'over pious.' "26
In autumn 1927 she gave a retreat to fifty women at Canter-
bury Cathedral.27 Many of her retreatants were also under her
spiritual direction. They too were becoming women lay leaders,
and Underhill — by the sheer force of her creative talent — was
changing the position of women in British churches. Many of
her retreats were later published, among these *Concerning the
Inner Life* (1926), *The House of the Soul* (1929), *The Golden Sequence* (1933), *The Mount of Purification* (1933), *The School of
Charity* (1934), and *Abba* (1934). *The Spiritual Life* (1937) was

based on four broadcast talks. Some retreats and talks went un-published in her lifetime but were later discovered and brought into print.[28]

Her full appreciation of the sacramental life is seen in her last major work, *Worship* (1937). *Worship* has the depth and scale — that is, the scope — of her first work, *Mysticism*. The book not only deals with liturgical life, but also with aspects of devotion which had become deeply important to Underhill: ado-ration, sacrifice, self-offering. In *Worship* she could finally present a whole vision of the spiritual life within a mature understanding of Christian faith and practice.

A final academic honor came to her in 1938. She had been the first woman to be invited to give a series of theological lectures at Oxford University (1921); she had been made a fellow of King's College, Cambridge, in 1928. In 1938 she received the degree of doctor of divinity from Aberdeen University.

The next year, 1939, war was again breaking out. Evelyn Underhill found that she could not support the war.

In the First World War she had taken an active citizen's role. She had spoken at meetings and worked in the Admiralty. But as war threatened again during the 1930s she found her views had changed. There was an active peace movement in Britain, and Underhill joined it. She declared herself a pacifist and became a leading figure in the Anglican Pacifist Fellowship. In their behalf she wrote, in an uncompromising pamphlet: "On the question of war between man and man she [the Church] cannot compro-mise."[29] Although she was inspired by the courage of the English at Dunkirk, she remained steadfast in her opinions even as the Second World War was beginning and England was under at-tack. On May 12, 1941, she wrote in a letter: "I think Hitler is a real 'scourge of God'... and there are only two ways of meet-ing him — war, or the Cross. And only a very small number are ready for the Cross, in the full sense of loving and unresisting abandonment to the worst that may come."[30] In a sense she was experiencing the Cross in another way; by this time her health was failing. She died from a cerebral hemorrhage on June 15,

1941. She was buried at St. John's Parish Church, Hampstead. Her husband, Hubert Stuart Moore, outlived her.

Hardly a remote or reclusive figure, Underhill practiced contemplation in the middle of a busy life. She was good company; lived in a comfortable middle-class house and ran an organized household; gave parties; took road trips with her husband; loved sailing and was an accomplished yachtswoman, who achieved the status of master mariner; was fond of cats. In her younger days she was known to accompany her husband in the sidecar of his motorcycle. Those who have read Virginia Woolf's novel *Mrs. Dalloway* can see in it a reflection of the London after World War I in which Mrs. Hubert Stuart Moore lived and entertained. However, there is a marked difference between Mrs. Stuart Moore and Mrs. Dalloway, namely, Evelyn's pronounced and passionate Christian faith.

Charles Williams reported how much Evelyn Underhill lived the devotional life as a matter of body and soul. Transforming effects upon her were noticed by some observers. One reported a "light" or "aureole" in her presence, during her last days when, suffering acutely from asthma, she refused all speaking engagements and public appearances.[31]

Underhill believed in and taught contemplative prayer as a gift within reach of any serious inquirer. Without question, she linked contemplation to what we must accomplish in the world. "More is required of those who wake up to reality, than the passive adoration of God or intimate communion with God." She insisted that those who pray must be active world-citizens: "Our place is not in the auditorium but the stage or, as the case may be, the field, workshop, study, laboratory because we ourselves form part of the creative apparatus of God, or at least are meant to form part of the creative apparatus of God. He made us in order to use us, and use us in the most profitable way; for His purpose, not ours. To live a spiritual life means subordinating all other interests to that single fact."[32]

Today Underhill's work continues to invite a broad audience of readers to full Christian devotion. Both men and women are attracted to her writing, and her major works are still in print. Yet Underhill is more than a writer on mysticism. She herself is a model of how the Christian life can be lived "in the middle of things." Decidedly a woman of our times, she opened new avenues for women's Christian leadership within very tradition-bound churches. She not only wrote about the spiritual life; she also lived it. Her life gives clear evidence of the transforming effects of prayer and spiritual discipline. She is a striking modern advocate of mysticism in everyday life.

Notes

1. Evelyn Underhill, *Practical Mysticism* (New York: E. P. Dutton, 1915, 1945), 30.

2. Ibid., 94.

3. Ibid., 94–95.

4. Christopher Armstrong, *Evelyn Underhill: An Introduction to Her Life and Writings* (Grand Rapids, Mich.: William B. Eerdmans, 1975), 9.

5. Charles Williams, ed., *The Letters of Evelyn Underhill* (Westminster, Md.: Christian Classics, 1989; original publication by Longmans, Green, 1943), 7. Williams knew Underhill personally. His introduction to this volume of her letters is of great value.

6. Armstrong, *Evelyn Underhill*, 17. Armstrong suggests this phase took place about 1905.

7. Ibid., 32.

8. Williams, *Letters*, 125.

9. See the excellent discussion of these early works by Dana Greene in her literary biography, *Evelyn Underhill: Artist of the Infinite* (New York: Crossroad, 1990), 21 and following. Williams, in his introduction to *The Letters of Evelyn Underhill*, already cited, also notes many flaws in Underhill's early fictional work.

10. Identified sometimes as *Pascendi Gregis*, an encyclical letter of Pope Pius X issued September 8, 1907. Together with the decree of the Holy Office entitled *Lamentabili* and the Oath against Modernism, the encyclical letter spearheaded the Roman Catholic condemnation of Modernism. See *New Catholic Encyclopedia*, 10:1048.

11. Letters from the baron to Underhill in January 1911 record this. See Margaret Cropper's biography, *Evelyn Underhill* (London: Longmans, Green, 1958), 40, and Greene's account, *Evelyn Underhill*, 44. *Mysti-*

cism appeared during the first week of March 1911. Later in the year, Evelyn wrote to her friend J. H. Herbert, expressing delight about her new acquaintance with Baron von Hügel (see Williams, *Letters,* 129).

12. See comments by Bernard McGinn in *Foundations of Mysticism: Origins to the Fifth Century* (New York: Crossroad, 1991), 293–96.

13. Greene, *Evelyn Underhill,,* 54–55. Greene also cites objections from Emma Herman, whose book *The Meaning and Value of Mysticism* appeared four years after Underhill's. Herman's objections were in the following vein: What is the mystic sense? Does everyone have it? Doesn't a theological formulation or belief-system about the Absolute make any difference to the mystic's experience? Doesn't Underhill's emphasis on union seem callous in view of human suffering and pain and the prevalence of evil and sin? Underhill answered her objections and von Hügel's in the preface to the 1930 edition of *Mysticism,* but without changing her primary focus.

14. For a detailed account of the Baron's comments and advice, see Armstrong, *Evelyn Underhill,* 133–35.

15. Cropper, *Evelyn Underhill,* 44. Both Margaret Cropper and Lucy Menzies knew Evelyn Underhill. Menzies was the warden at Pleshey retreat house. The Cropper biography incorporates much of Lucy Menzies's unfinished biography of Underhill.

16. Harvey D. Egan, S.J., *Christian Mysticism: The Future of a Tradition* (New York: Pueblo Publishing Company, 1984), 7.

17. Ibid., 7–8.

18. Evelyn Underhill, *Mysticism* (New York: Doubleday, 1990), 85.

19. McGinn provides a brief assessment of Underhill in his already cited *Foundations of Mysticism,* 273–75.

20. I am indebted to Harvey Egan, *Christian Mysticism,* 8.

21. Evelyn Underhill, "Bergson and the Mystics," *Living Age* 27 (February 10, 1912): 511–22.

22. Evelyn Underhill, "An Indian Mystic," review of *Gitanjali* by R. Tagore, *The Nation* (November 12, 1912): 321. Cited by Greene in *Evelyn Underhill,* 57–58.

23. Williams, *Letters,* 178.

24. Cropper cites a letter to Evelyn Underhill from the baron, dated October 29, 1921, in which he lays out his very nuanced view of the matter. It seems he is more concerned about the particulars of Evelyn's spiritual life than whether she becomes a Catholic. Also, she should not become Catholic without receiving a definite "call." And he alludes to difficulties of obedience placed upon Roman Catholics (Cropper, *Evelyn Underhill,* 69).

25. This account is given by Charles Williams in his introduction to *Letters*, 26. Williams is drawing from a letter which he does not include in the volume.

26. Quoted in Cropper, *Evelyn Underhill*, 159.

27. Ibid., 161–62.

28. Grace Brame has edited four of Underhill's retreats under the title *The Ways of the Spirit* (New York: Crossroad, 1990).

29. Williams, *Letters*, 41.

30. Armstrong, *Evelyn Underhill*, 288.

31. Williams, *Letters*, 37. Williams quotes an account by an unidentified friend of a first meeting with Evelyn Underhill at her Camden Square home in 1937, shortly after one of her bouts of bad illness. This person saw Underhill as transfigured.

32. Evelyn Underhill, *The Spiritual Life* (New York: Harper & Row, 1937), 84–85.

1

The Spiritual Life

One good way to begin with Underhill is in her shorter works. In these she defines and describes the spiritual life. Among the most engaging are Practical Mysticism *and* The Spiritual Life, *the latter adapted from four broadcast talks. Notice her colloquial style and vivid word-pictures. Underhill is inviting her readers to sample the spiritual life. In these short, popular treatises, Underhill opens up the possibility of learning from the mystics and tasting the joy of God's presence in the middle of things.*

WHAT IS MYSTICISM?

Those who are interested in that special attitude towards the universe which is now loosely called "mystical," find themselves beset by a multitude of persons who are constantly asking — some with real fervor, some with curiosity, and some with disdain — "What is mysticism?" When referred to the writings of the mystics themselves, and to other works in which this question appears to be answered, these people reply that such books are wholly incomprehensible to them.

On the other hand, the genuine inquirer will find before long a number of self-appointed apostles who are eager to answer his question in many strange and inconsistent ways, calculated to increase rather than resolve the obscurity of his mind. He will learn that mysticism is a philosophy, an illusion, a kind of religion, a disease; that it means having visions, performing conjuring tricks, leading an idle, dreamy, and selfish life, neglecting one's business, wallowing in vague spiritual emotions, and being in tune with the infinite. He will discover that it emancipates him from all dogmas — sometimes from all morality — and at the same time that it is very superstitious. One expert tells him that it is simply "Catholic piety," another that Walt Whitman was a typical mystic; a third assures him that all mysticism comes from the East, and supports his statement by an appeal to the mango trick. At the end of a prolonged series of lectures, sermons, tea-parties, and talks with earnest persons, the inquirer is still heard saying too often in tones of exasperation — "What *is* mysticism?"

I dare not pretend to solve a problem which has provided so much good hunting in the past. It is indeed the object of this little essay to persuade the practical man to the one satisfactory course: that of discovering the answer for himself. Yet perhaps it will give confidence if I confess at the outset that I have discovered a definition which to me appears to cover all the ground; or at least, all that part of the ground which is worth covering. It will hardly stretch to the mango trick; but it finds room at once for the visionaries and philosophers, for Walt Whitman and the saints:

Here is the definition:

Mysticism is the art of union with Reality. The mystic is a person who has attained that union in greater or less degree; or who aims at and believes in such attainment.

It is not expected that the inquirer will find great comfort in this sentence when it first meets his eye. The ultimate question, "What is Reality?" — a question, perhaps, which never occurred to him before — is already forming in his mind; and he knows it will cause him infinite distress. Only a mystic can answer it: and he, in terms which other mystics alone will understand. Therefore, for the time being, the practical man may put it on one side. All that he is asked to consider now is this: that the word "union" represents not so much a rare and unimaginable operation, as something which he is doing, in a vague, imperfect fashion, at every moment of his conscious life; and doing with intensity and thoroughness in all the more valid moments of that life. We know a thing only by uniting with it; by assimilating it; by an interpenetration of it and ourselves. It gives itself to us, just in so far as we give ourselves to it; and it is because our outflow towards things is always so perfunctory and so languid, that our comprehension of things is so perfunctory and languid too. The great Sufi who said, "Pilgrimage to the place of the wise, is to escape the flame of separation" spoke the literal truth. Wisdom is the fruit of communion; ignorance the inevitable portion of those who "keep themselves to themselves," and stand apart, judging, analyzing the things which they have never truly known.

Because he has surrendered himself to it, "united" with it, the patriot knows his country, the artist knows the subject of his art, the lover his beloved, the saint his God, in a manner which is inconceivable as well as unattainable by the looker-on. Real knowledge, since it always implies an intuitive sympathy more or less intense, is far more accurately suggested by the symbols of touch and taste than by those of hearing and sight. True, analytic thought follows swiftly upon the contact, the apprehension, the union: and we, in our muddle-headed way, have persuaded ourselves that this is the essential part of knowledge — that it is, in fact, more important to cook the hare than to catch it. But when we get rid of this illusion and go back to the more primitive activities through which our mental kitchen gets its supplies, we see that the distinction between mystic and non-mystic is not merely that between the rationalist and the dreamer, between intellect and intuition. The question which divides them is really this: What, out of the mass of material offered to it, shall consciousness seize upon — with what aspects of the universe shall it "unite"?

It is notorious that the operations of the average human consciousness unite the self, not with things as they really are, but with images, notions, aspects of things. The verb "to be," which he uses so lightly, does not truly apply to any of the objects amongst which the practical man supposes himself to dwell. For him the hare of Reality is always ready-jugged: he conceives not the living, lovely, wild, swift-moving creature which has been sacrificed in order that he may be fed on the deplorable dish which he calls "things as they really are." So complete, indeed, is the separation of his consciousness from the facts of being, that he feels no sense of loss. He is happy enough "understanding," garnishing, assimilating the carcass from which the principle of life and growth has been ejected, and whereof only the most digestible portions have been retained. He is not "mystical."

•

We now begin to attach at least a fragmentary meaning to the statement that "mysticism is the art of union with Reality." We see that the claim of such a poet as Whitman to be a mystic lies in the fact that he has achieved a passionate communion with the deeper levels of life than those with which we usually deal — has thrust past the current notion to the Fact: that the claim of such a saint as Teresa is bound up with her declaration that she has achieved union with the Divine Essence itself. The visionary is a mystic when his vision mediates to him an actuality beyond the reach of the senses. The philosopher is a mystic when he passes beyond thought to the pure apprehension of the truth. The active man is a mystic when he knows his actions to be part of a greater activity. Blake, Plotinus, Joan of Arc, and John of the Cross — there is a link which binds all these together: but if he is to make use of it, the inquirer must find that link for himself. All four exhibit different forms of the working of the contemplative consciousness; a faculty which is proper to all men, though few take the trouble to develop it. Their attention to life has changed its character, sharpened its focus: and as a result they see, some a wider landscape, some a more brilliant, more significant, more detailed world than that which is apparent to the less educated, less observant vision of common sense.   — *Practical Mysticism*

WHAT IS THE SPIRITUAL LIFE?

"The Spiritual Life" is a dangerously ambiguous term; indeed, it would be interesting to know what meaning any one reader at the present moment is giving to these three words. Many, I am afraid, would really be found to mean "the life of my own inside": and a further section, to mean something very holy, difficult, and peculiar — a sort of honors course in personal religion — to which they did not intend to aspire.

Both these kinds of individualist — the people who think of the spiritual life as something which is for themselves and about themselves, and the people who regard it as something which is not for themselves — seem to need a larger horizon, within which these interesting personal facts can be placed; and seen in rather truer proportion. Any spiritual view which focuses attention on ourselves, and puts the human creature with its small ideas and adventures in the center foreground, is dangerous till we recognize its absurdity. So at least we will try to get away from these petty notions, and make a determined effort to see our situation within that great spiritual landscape which is so much too great for our limited minds to grasp, and yet is our true inheritance — a present reality here and now, within which our real lives are now being lived. We will look at it through the wide-angle lens of disinterested worship; and put aside those useful little pince-nez which bring into sharp focus our own qualities, desires, interests, and difficulties, but blur everything else....

So many Christians are like deaf people at a concert. They study the program carefully, believe every statement made in it, speak respectfully of the quality of the music, but only really hear a phrase now and again. So they have no notion at all of the mighty symphony which fills the universe, to which our lives are destined to make their tiny contribution, and which is the self-expression of the Eternal God.

Yet there are plenty of things in our normal experience, which imply the existence of that world, that music, that life. If, for instance, we consider the fact of prayer, the almost universal impulse to seek and appeal to a power beyond ourselves, and notice the heights to which it can rise in those who give themselves to it with courage and love — the power it exerts, the heroic vocations and costly sacrifices which it supports, the transformations of character which it effects — it is a sufficiently mysterious characteristic of man.... No one who studies with sympathy, for instance, the history of religious revivals, can doubt that here, often in a grotesque and unlovely disguise, a force from beyond the world really breaks in upon the temporal order with disconcerting power.

So, too, all who are sensitive to beauty know the almost agonizing sense of revelation its sudden impact brings — the abrupt disclosure of the mountain summit, the wild cherry-tree in blossom, the crowning moment of a great concerto, witnessing to another beauty beyond sense. And again, any mature person looking back on their own past life, will be forced to recognize factors in that life, which cannot be attributed to heredity, environment, opportunity, personal initiative, or mere chance.... It is as if a hidden directive power, personal, living, free, were working through circumstances and often against our intention or desire; pressing us in a certain direction, and molding us to a certain design.

•

Life in its fullness, the life which shall develop and use all our capacities and fulfil all our possibilities, must involve correspondence not only with our visible and ever-changing, but also with our invisible and unchanging environment: the Spirit of all spirits, God, in whom we live and move and have our being. The significance, the greatness of humanity, consists in our ability to do this. The meaning of our life is bound up with the meaning of the universe....

When we consider our situation like that, when we lift our eyes from the crowded by-pass to the eternal hills; then, how much the personal and practical things we have to deal with are enriched. What meaning and coherence come into our scattered lives. We mostly spend those lives conjugating three verbs: to Want, to Have, and to Do. Craving, clutching, and fussing, on the material, political, social, emotional, intellectual — even on the religious — plane, we are kept in perpetual unrest: forgetting that none of these verbs have any ultimate significance, except so far as they are transcended by and included in, the fundamental verb, to Be: and that Being, not wanting, having, and doing, is the essence of a spiritual life. But now, with this widening of the horizon, our personal ups and downs, desires, cravings, efforts, are seen in scale; as small and transitory spiritual facts, within a vast, abiding spiritual world, and lit by a steady spiritual light. And at once a new coherence comes into our existence, a new tranquillity and release. Like a chalet in the Alps, that homely existence gains atmosphere, dignity, significance from the greatness of the sky above it and the background of the everlasting hills.

The people of our time are helpless, distracted, and rebellious, unable to interpret that which is happening, and full of apprehension about that which is to come, largely because they have lost this sure hold on the eternal; which gives to each life meaning and direction, and with meaning and direction gives steadiness. I do not mean by this a mere escape from our problems and dangers, a slinking away from the actual to enjoy the eternal. I mean an acceptance and living out of the actual, in its homeliest details and its utmost demands, in the light of the eternal; and with that peculiar sense of ultimate security which only a hold on the eternal brings.

•

This, of course, is what religion is about; this adherence to God, this confident dependence on that which is unchanging. This is the more abundant life, which in its own particular language and own particular way, it calls us to live.... This view of our situation fills us with a certain awed and humble gladness. It delivers us from all niggling fuss about ourselves, prevents us from feeling self-important about our own little spiritual adventures; and yet makes them worth while as part of one great spiritual adventure.

It means, when we come down again to our own particular case, that my spiritual life is not something specialized and intense; a fenced-off devotional patch rather difficult to cultivate, and needing to be sheltered from the cold winds of the outer world. Nor is it an alternative to my outward, practical life. On the contrary, it is the very source of that quality and purpose which makes my practical life worth while. The practical life of a vast number of people is not, as a matter of fact, worth while at all. It is like an impressive fur coat with no one inside it. One sees many of these coats occupying positions of great responsibility. Hans Andersen's story of the king with no clothes told one bitter and common truth about human nature; but the story of the clothes with no king describes a situation just as common and even more pitiable.

Still less does the spiritual life mean a mere cultivation of one's own soul; poking about our interior premises with an electric torch. Even though in its earlier stages it may, and generally does, involve dealing with ourselves, and that in a drastic way, and therefore requires personal effort and personal choice, it is also intensely social; for it is a life that is shared with all other spirits, whether in the body or out of the body, to adopt St. Paul's words. You remember how Dante says that directly a soul ceases to say Mine, and says Ours, it makes the transition from the narrow, constricted, individual life to the truly free, truly personal, truly creative spiritual life; in which all are linked together in one single response to the Father of all spirits, God. . . . Every advance made by one is made for all.

Only when we recognize all this and act on it, are we fully alive and taking our proper place in the universe of spirits; for life means the fullest possible give and take between the living creature and its environment: breathing, feeding, growing, changing. And spiritual life, which is profoundly organic, means the give and take, the willed correspondence of the little human spirit with the Infinite Spirit, here where it is; its feeding upon Him, its growth towards perfect union with Him, its response to His attraction and subtle pressure. That growth and that response may seem to us like a movement, a journey, in which by various unexpected and often unattractive paths, we are drawn almost in spite of ourselves — not as a result of our own over-anxious struggles — to the real end of our being, the place where we are ordained to be....

There are countless ways in which this may happen: sometimes under conditions which seem to the world like the very frustration of life, of progress, of growth. Thus boundless initiative is chained to a sick bed and transmuted into sacrifice; the lover of beauty is sent to serve in the slum, the lover of stillness is kept on the run all day, the sudden demand to leave all comes to the one who least expects it, and through and in these apparent frustrations the life of the spirit emerges, and grows....

St. Paul did not want to be an apostle to the Gentiles. He wanted to be a clever and appreciated young Jewish scholar, and kicked against the pricks. St. Ambrose and St. Augustine did not want to be overworked and worried bishops. Nothing was farther from their intention. St. Cuthbert wanted the solitude and freedom of his hermitage on the Farne; but he did not often get there. St. Francis Xavier's preference was for an ordered life close to his beloved master, St. Ignatius. At a few hours notice he was sent out to be the Apostle of the Indies and never returned to Europe again. Henry Martyn, the fragile and exquisite scholar, was compelled to sacrifice the intellectual life to which he was so perfectly fitted for the missionary life to which he felt he was decisively called. In all these, a power beyond themselves decided the direction of life. Yet in all we recognize not frustration, but the highest of all types of achievement.

•

The first question here, then, is not "What is best for my soul?" nor is it even "What is most useful to humanity?" But — transcending both these limited aims — what function must this life fulfil in the great and secret economy of God?...

Indeed, if God is All and His Word to us is All, that must mean that He is the reality and controlling factor of every situation, religious or secular; and that it is only for His glory and creative purpose that it exists. Therefore our favorite distinction between the spiritual life and the practical life is false. We cannot divide them. One affects the other all the time: for we are creatures of sense and of spirit, and must live an amphibious life. Christ's whole Ministry was an exhibition, first in one way and then in another, of this mysterious truth.... For a spiritual life is simply a life in which all that we do comes from the center, where we are anchored in God: a life soaked through and through by a sense of His reality and claim, and self-giver, to the great movement of His will.

Most of our conflicts and difficulties come from trying to deal with the spiritual and practical aspects of our life separately instead of realizing them as parts of one whole....

There is no real occasion for tumult, strain, conflict, anxiety, once we have reached the living conviction that God is All. All takes place within Him, He alone matters, He alone is. Our spiritual life is His affair; because, whatever we may think to the contrary, it is really produced by His steady attraction, and our humble and self-forgetful response to it. It consists in being drawn, at His pace and in His way, to the place where He wants us to be; not the place we fancied for ourselves.

Some people may seem to us to go to God by a moving staircase; where they can assist matters a bit by their own efforts, but much gets done for them and progress does not cease. Some appear to be whisked past us in a lift; whilst we find ourselves on a steep flight of stairs with a bend at the top, so that we cannot see how much farther we have to go. But none of this really matters; what matters is the conviction that all are moving towards God, and, in that journey, accompanied, supported, checked, and fed by God. Since our dependence on Him is absolute, and our desire is that His Will shall be done, this great desire can gradually swallow up, neutralize all our small self-centered desires. When that happens life, inner and outer, becomes one single, various act of adoration and self-giving; one undivided response of the creature to the demand and pressure of Creative Love.

— The Spiritual Life

THE SPIRITUAL LIFE AS CO-OPERATION WITH GOD

More is required of those who wake up to reality, than the passive adoration of God or intimate communion with God. Those purposes, great as they are, do not cover the purpose of our creation. The riches and beauty of the spiritual landscape are not disclosed to us in order that we may sit in the sun parlor, be grateful for the excellent hospitality, and contemplate the glorious view. Some people suppose that the spiritual life mainly consists in doing that. God provides the spectacle. We gaze with reverent appreciation from our comfortable seats, and call this proceeding Worship.

No idea of our situation could be more mistaken than this. Our place is not in the auditorium but the stage — or, as the case may be, the field, workshop, study, laboratory — because we ourselves form part of the creative apparatus of God, or at least are meant to form part of the creative apparatus of God. He made us in order to use us, and use us in the most profitable way; for His purpose, not ours. To live a spiritual life means subordinating all other interests to that single fact. Sometimes our position seems to be that of tools; taken up when wanted, used in ways which we had not expected for an object on which our opinion was not asked, and then laid down. Sometimes we are the currency used in some great operation, of which the purpose is not revealed to us. Sometimes we are servants, left year in, year out to the same monotonous job. Sometimes we are conscious fellow-workers with the Perfect, striving to bring the Kingdom in. But whatever our particular place or job may be, it means the austere conditions of the workshop, not the free-lance activities of the messy but well-meaning amateur; clocking in at the right time and tending the machine in the right way. Sometimes, perhaps, carrying on for years with a machine we do not very well understand and do not enjoy; because it needs doing, and no one else is available. Or accepting a situation quite quietly, when a job that we felt we were managing excellently is taken away. Taking responsibility if we are called to it, or just bringing the workers their dinner, cleaning and sharpening the tools. All self-willed choices and obstinacy drained out of what we thought to be our work; so that it becomes more and more God's work in us.

•

I go back to the one perfect summary of man's Godward life and call — the Lord's Prayer. Consider how dynamic and purposive is its character. Thy Will be *done* — Thy Kingdom *come!* There is energy, drive, purpose in these words; an intensity of desire — for the coming of perfection into life. . . . It is useless to utter fervent petitions for that Kingdom to be established and that Will to be done, unless we are willing to do something about it ourselves. As we walk through London we know very well that we are not walking through the capital of the Kingdom of Heaven. Yet we might be, if the conviction and action of every Christian in London were set without any conditions or any reluctance towards this end; if there were perfect consistency, whatever it cost — and it is certain the cost would not be small — between our spiritual ideals and our social and political acts.

We are agents of the Creative Spirit in this world. Real advance in the spiritual life, then, means accepting this vocation with all it involves. . . .

So now we come back to this ordinary mixed life of every day, in which we find ourselves — the life of house and work, tube and tram, newspaper and cinema, with its tangle of problems and suggestions and demands — and consider what we are to do about that; how, within its homely limitations, we can co-operate with the Will. It is far easier, though not very easy, to develop and preserve a spiritual outlook on life, than it is to make our everyday actions harmonize with that spiritual outlook. . . . This will be decisive for the way we behave as to our personal, social, and national obligations. It will decide the papers we read, the movements we support, the kind of administrators we vote for, our attitude to social and international justice. For though we may renounce the world for ourselves, refuse the attempt to get anything out of it, we have to accept it as the sphere in which we are to co-operate with the Spirit, and try to do the Will. Therefore the prevalent notion that spirituality and politics have nothing to do with one another is the exact opposite of the truth. Once it is accepted in a realistic sense, the Spiritual Life has everything to do with politics. It means that certain convictions about God and the world become the moral and spiritual imperatives of our life; and this must be decisive for the way we choose to behave....

The life of this planet, and especially its human life, is a life in which something has gone wrong, and badly wrong. Every time that we see an unhappy face, an unhealthy body, hear a bitter or despairing word, we are reminded of that. The occasional dazzling flashes of pure beauty, pure goodness, pure love which show us what God wants and what He is, only throw into more vivid relief the horror of cruelty, greed, oppression, hatred, ugliness.... Unless we put on blinkers, we can hardly avoid seeing all this; and unless we are warmly wrapped up in our own cozy ideas, and absorbed in our own interests, we surely cannot help feeling the sense of obligation, the shame of acquiescence, the call to do something about it. To say day by day "Thy Kingdom Come" — if these tremendous words really stand for a conviction and desire does not mean "I quite hope that some day the Kingdom of God will be established, and peace and goodwill prevail. But at present I don't see how it is to be managed or what I can do about it." On the contrary, it means, or should mean, "Here am I! Send me!" — active, costly collaboration with the Spirit in whom we believe.

•

The action may be almost anything; from the ceaseless self-offering of the enclosed nun to the creation of beauty, or the clearance of slums. "Here am I! Send me!" means going anyhow, anywhere, at any time. Not where the prospects are good, but where the need is great; not to the obviously suitable job, which I'm sure that I can do with distinction; but to do the difficult thing, or give the unpopular message, in the uncongenial place. "And Moses said, Who am I, that I should go to Pharaoh and bring forth the children of Israel out of Egypt?" But he did it. Indeed, it is a peculiarity of the great spiritual personality that he or she constantly does in the teeth of circumstances what other people say cannot be done. He is driven by a total devotion which overcomes all personal timidity, and gives a power unknown to those who are playing for their own hand or carving their own career.

If we consider the lives of the Saints, we see the strange paths along which they were driven by the Will to the accomplishment of their destiny: how unexpected and uncongenial were the ways in which they were used to bring the Kingdom in and do the Will of God: and how the heavenly Bread which they were given was given to make them strong for this destiny, and not because it tasted nice. Great courage and initiative, the hardy endurance of privation and fatigue, the calm acceptance of unpopularity, misunderstanding, and contempt, are at least as characteristic of them as any of the outward marks of piety. So too their inner life, which we are inclined to think of as a constant succession of spiritual delights, was often hard and painful. Willingly and perpetually, they prayed from within the Cross, shared the agony, darkness, loneliness of the Cross; and because of this, they shared in its saving power.

The Church is in the world to save the world. It is a tool of God for that purpose; not a comfortable religious club established in fine historical premises. Every one of its members is required, in one way or another, to co-operate with the Spirit in working for that great end: and much of this work will be done in secret and invisible ways. We are transmitters as well as receivers. Our contemplation and our action, our humble self-opening to God, keeping ourselves sensitive to His music and light, and our generous self-opening to our fellow creatures, keeping ourselves sensitive to their needs, ought to form one life; mediating between God and His world, and bringing the saving power of the Eternal into time.

We are far from realizing all that human spirits can do for one another on spiritual levels if they will pay the price; how truly and really our souls interpenetrate, and how impossible and un-Christian it is to "keep ourselves to ourselves." When St. Catherine of Siena used to say to the sinners who came to her: "Have no fear, I will take the burden of your sins," she made a practical promise, which she fulfilled literally and at her own great cost. She could do this because she was totally self-given to the purposes of the Spirit, was possessed by the Divine passion of saving love, and so had taken her place in the great army of rescuing souls.

•

St. John of the Cross says that every quality or virtue which that Spirit really produces in men's souls has three distinguishing characters — as it were a threefold National Mark — Tranquility, Gentleness, Strength. All our action — and now we are thinking specially of action — must be peaceful, gentle, and strong. That suggests, doesn't it? an immense depth, and an invulnerable steadiness as the soul's abiding temper; a depth and a steadiness which come from the fact that our small action is now part of the total action of God, whose Spirit, as another saint has said, "works always in tranquillity." Fuss and feverishness, anxiety, intensity, intolerance, instability, pessimism . . . every kind of hurry and worry — these, even on the highest levels, are signs of the self-made and self-acting soul; the spiritual parvenu. The saints are never like that. . . .

If, then, we desire a simple test of the quality of our spiritual life, a consideration of the tranquility, gentleness, and strength with which we deal with the circumstances of our outward life will serve us better than anything that is based on the loftiness of our religious notions, or fervor of our religious feelings. It is a test that can be applied anywhere and at any time. Tranquillity, gentleness, and strength, carrying us through the changes of weather, the ups and downs of the route, the varied surface of the road; the inequalities of family life, emotional and professional disappointments, the sudden intervention of bad fortune or bad health, the rising and falling of our religious temperature. This is the threefold imprint of the Spirit on the souls surrendered to His great action.

We see that plainly in the Saints; in the quiet steadiness of spirit with which they meet the vicissitudes and sufferings of their lives. They know that these small and changing lives, about which we are often so troubled, are part of a greater mystery; the life that is related to God and known by God....

•

It is here that we recognize their real character; as various expressions in action of one life, based on one conviction and desire. Thus there is no tendency to snatch another's work, or dodge dull bits of their own; no cheapening sense of hurry, or nervous anxiety about success. The action of those whose lives are given to the Spirit has in it something of the leisure of Eternity; and because of this, they achieve far more than those whose lives are enslaved by the rush and hurry, the unceasing tick-tick of the world. In the spiritual life it is very important to get our timing right. Otherwise we tend to forget that God, Who is greater than our heart, is greater than our job too.

We have considered that co-operation with the Spirit's action ...as a giving of ourselves to His service, doing some of His work in the world. But there is another and deeper side: the hidden action of each soul called by God, the effort and struggle of the interior life what *we* have to do in response to the Love which is drawing us out of darkness into His great light. Even that mysterious communion with God in which we seek, and offer ourselves to, that which we love — in spite of the deep peace it brings — is not without the pain and tension which must be felt by imperfect creatures when they contemplate and stretch towards a beauty and perfection which they cannot reach. . . .

The Perfection at which the awakened soul gazes is a magnet, drawing him towards itself. It means effort, faithfulness, courage, and sometimes grim encounters if he is to respond to that attraction, and move towards it along the narrow track which leads up and out from the dark valleys of the mind. . . .

Always looking the same way, and always moving the same way: in spite of obstacles, discouragements, mockery, and fatigue. "Thou has made us for thyself, and our hearts find no rest save in thee." But we must be willing to undertake the journey, whatever it may cost.   — *The Spiritual Life*

2

The House of the Soul

In her book The House of the Soul *Evelyn Underhill borrows a creative approach from earlier mystical writers. She chooses a single powerful image and explores it thoroughly, as Teresa of Avila had done, for example, in* The Interior Castle. *In the readings that follow, notice the many homely touches. Underhill's romantic and poetic streak is being offset by the ordinary and the everyday. She considers such virtues as Prudence, Temperance, and Fortitude with the vocabulary of good housekeeping. Her goal is to place spiritual life in the middle of things. Bear in mind, as you read, that the two-storied house (her central figure) is in line with a theological understanding that grace builds on nature, that body is completed by soul.*

THE SOUL'S HOUSE: NOT TOO BIG AN IDEA

The soul's house, that interior dwelling-place which we all possess, for the upkeep of which we are responsible — a place in which we can meet God, or from which in a sense we can exclude God — that is not too big an idea for us. Though no imagery drawn from the life of sense can ever be adequate to the strange and delicate contacts, tensions, demands, and benedictions of the life that lies beyond sense: though the important part of every parable is that which it fails to express: still, here is a conception which can be made to cover many of the truths that govern the interior life of prayer.

First, we are led to consider the position of the house. However interesting and important its peculiarities may seem to the tenant, it is not as a matter of fact an unusually picturesque and interesting mansion made to an original design, and set in its own grounds with no other building in sight. Christian spirituality knows nothing of this sort of individualism. It insists that we do not inhabit detached residences, but are parts of a vast spiritual organism; that even the most hidden life is never lived for itself alone. Our soul's house forms part of the vast City of God. Though it may not be an important mansion with a frontage on the main street, nevertheless it shares all the obligations and advantages belonging to the city as a whole....

It is true that God creates souls in a marvelous liberty and variety.... It is true also, that the furnishing of our rooms and cultivation of our garden is largely left to our personal industry and good taste. Still, in a general way, we must fall in with the city's plan; and consider, when we hang some new and startling curtains, how they will look from the street.... So into all the affairs of the little house there should enter a certain sense of the city, and beyond this of the infinite world in which the city stands: some awe-struck memory of our double situation, at once so homely and so mysterious. We must each maintain unimpaired our unique relation with God; yet without forgetting our intimate contact with the rest of the city, or the mesh of invisible life which binds all the inhabitants in one.

For it is on the unchanging Life of God, as on a rock, that the whole city is founded. That august and cherishing Spirit is the atmosphere which bathes it, and fills each room of every little house — quickening, feeding, and sustaining. He is the one Reality which makes us real; and, equally, the other houses too. "If I am not in Thee, said St. Augustine, then I am not at all." We are often urged to think of the spiritual life as a personal adventure, a ceaseless hustle forward; with all its meaning condensed in the "perfection" of the last stage. But though progress, or rather growth, is truly in it, such growth in so far as it is real can only arise from, and be conditioned by, a far more fundamental relation — the growing soul's abidingness in God.

•

Next, what type of house does the soul live in? It is a two-story house. The psychologist too often assumes that it is a one-roomed cottage with a mud floor; and never even attempts to go upstairs. The extreme transcendentalist sometimes talks as though it were perched in the air, like the lake dwellings of our primitive ancestors, and had no ground floor at all. A more humble attention to facts suggests that neither of these simplifications is true. We know that we have a ground floor, a natural life biologically conditioned, with animal instincts and affinities; and that this life is very important, for it is the product of the divine creativity — its builder and maker is God. But we know too that we have an upper floor, a supernatural life, with supernatural possibilities, a capacity for God; and that this, man's peculiar prerogative, is more important still. If we try to live on one floor alone we destroy the mysterious beauty of our human vocation; so utterly a part of the fugitive and creaturely life of this planet and yet so deeply colored by Eternity; so entirely one with the world of nature, and yet, in the Spirit, a habitation of God. Thou madest him lower than the angels, to crown him with glory and worship. We are created both in Time and in Eternity, not truly one but truly two; and every thought, word, and act must be subdued to the dignity of that double situation in which Almighty God has placed and companions the childish spirit of man....

But the soul's house will never be a real home, unless the ground floor is as cared for and as habitable as the beautiful rooms upstairs. We are required to live in the whole of our premises, and are responsible for the condition of the whole of our premises. It is useless to repaper the drawing-room, if what we really need is a new sink. In that secret Divine purpose which is drawing all life toward perfection, the whole house is meant to be beautiful, and ought to be beautiful; for it comes from God, and was made to His design. Christ's soul when on earth lived in one of these houses; had to use the same fitments, make the same arrangements do. We cannot excuse our own failures by attributing them to the inconvenience of the premises, and the fact that some very old-fashioned bits of apparatus survive. Most of us have inherited some ugly bits of furniture, or unfortunate family portraits which we can't get rid of, and which prevent our rooms being quite a success. Nevertheless the soul does not grow strong merely by enjoying its upstairs privileges, and ignoring downstairs disadvantages, problems, and responsibilities; but only by tackling its real task of total transformation. It is called to maintain a house which shall be in its completeness a habitation of God in the Spirit; subdued to His purposes on all levels, manifesting His glory in what we call natural life, as well as in what we call spiritual life. For man is the link between these two orders; truly created a little lower than the angels, yet truly crowned with glory and worship, because in this unperfected human nature the Absolute Life itself has deigned to dwell.

That means, reduced to practice, that the whole house with its manifold and graded activities must be a house of prayer. It does not mean keeping a Quiet Room to which we can retreat, with mystical pictures on the walls, and curtains over the windows to temper the disconcerting intensity of the light.... Are we capable of the adventure of courage which inspires the great prayer of St. Augustine: "The house of my soul is narrow; do Thou enter in and enlarge it! It is ruinous; do Thou repair it"? Can we risk the visitation of the mysterious Power that will go through all our untidy rooms, showing up their shortcomings and their possibilities; reproving by the tranquillity of order the waste and muddle of our inner life?...

The Lord's Prayer, in which St. Teresa said that she found the whole art of contemplation from its simple beginning to its transcendent goal, witnesses with a wonderful beauty and completeness to this two-story character of the soul's house; and yet its absolute unity. It begins at the top, in the watch tower of faith, with the sublime assertion of our supernatural status the one

relation, intimate yet inconceivable, that governs all the rest —
"Our Father who art in Heaven, hallowed be *Thy* name...."

Thence, step by step, this prayer brings us downstairs, goes
with us through the whole house; bringing the supernatural into
the natural, blessing and sanctifying, cleansing and rectifying
every aspect of the home. "*Thy* Kingdom come!" Hope — trustful expectation. "*Thy* will be done!" Charity — the loving union
of our wills with the Infinite Will. Then the ground floor. "Give
us this day" — that food from beyond ourselves which nourishes
and sustains our life. Forgive all our little failures and excesses,
neutralize the corroding power of our conflicts, disharmonies, rebellions, sins. We can't deal with them alone. Teach us, as toward
our fellow citizens, to share that generous tolerance of God. Lead
us not into situations where we are tried beyond our strength; but
meet us on the battlefield of personality, and protect the weak-
ness of the adolescent spirit against the downward pull of the
inhabitants of the lower floor.

And then, the reason of all this; bringing together, in one
supreme declaration of joy and confidence, the soul's sense of that
supporting, holy, and eternal Reality who is the Ruler and the
Light of the city, and of every room in every little house. *Thine* is
the Kingdom, the Power, and the Glory. If our interior life be subdued to the spirit of this prayer, with its rich sense of our mighty
heritage and child-like status, our total dependence on the Reality
of God, then the soul's house is truly running well. Its action is
transfused by contemplation. The door is open between the upper
and the lower floor; the life of spirit and life of sense.

"Two cities," said St. Augustine, "have been created by two
loves: the earthly city by love of self even to contempt of God,
the heavenly city by love of God even to contempt of self. The
one city glories in itself; the other city glories in the Lord. The
one city glories in its own strength; the other city says to its God,
'I will love Thee, O Lord my strength.'" Perhaps there has never
been a time in Christian history when that contrast has been
more sharply felt than it is now — the contrast between that view
of man's situation and meaning, in which the emphasis falls on

humanity, its vast desires and wonderful achievements, even to contempt of God; and the view in which the emphasis falls on God's transcendent action and over-ruling will, even to contempt of self. St. Augustine saw, and still would see, mankind ever at work building those two cities; and every human soul as a potential citizen of one or the other. And from this point of view, that which we call the "interior life" is just the home life of those who inhabit the invisible City of God.

•

These free gifts of the supernatural are offered to each house; and only as free gifts can they be had. Our noisy little engine will not produce the true light; nor our most desperate digging a proper water supply. Recognition of this fact, this entire dependence of the creature, is essential if the full benefits of our mysterious citizenship are ever to be enjoyed by us. "I saw," said the poet of the Apocalypse, "the holy city coming *down* from God out of heaven... the glory of God lit it... the water of life proceeded out of the throne of God." All is the free gift of the supernatural; not the result of human growth and effort. God's generous and life-giving work in the world of souls ever goes before man's work in God. So the main thing about the Invisible City is not the industry and good character of the inhabitants: they do not make it shine. It is the tranquil operation, of that perpetual providence, which incites and supports their small activities; the direct and child-like relation in which they stand to the city's Ruler; the generous light and air that bathe the little houses; the unchanging rock of Eternity on which their foundations stand.

— The House of the Soul

THE GROUND FLOOR:
A WELL-ORDERED NATURAL LIFE

We come back to examine more closely our domestic responsibilities: the two floors of the soul's house. We begin on the ground floor; for until that is in decent order, it is useless to go upstairs. A well-ordered natural life is the only safe basis of our supernatural life: Christianity, which brought the ground floor, with its powerful but unruly impulses, within the area of God's grace, demands its sublimation and dedication to His purposes. We are required to live in the whole of our house, learning to go freely and constantly up and down stairs, backwards and forwards, easily and willingly, from one kind of life to the other; weaving together the higher and lower powers of the soul, and using both for the glory of God. No exclusive spirituality will serve the purposes of man, called to a link between two worlds....

Then the force of the ancient Advent prayer comes home to us. "O Wisdom proceeding out of the mouth of the Most High, come and teach me the way of Prudence" between the two conflicting aspects of my double life....

We owe to St. Thomas the noblest and deepest of all definitions of Prudence. For him, all virtues, all the soul's sources of energy, are forms and expressions of one thing — Love, the self's will and desire, in the ascending degrees of preference, interest, longing and devotedness, set towards God and the will of God....

Prudence is like a good housekeeper; not very attractive at first sight, but a valuable sort of woman to put in charge if you want your soul's house to be well run. With her eye on efficiency, but always for love's sake, she will use her resources in the best way, keep up the premises, provide regular and suitable meals. She will not serve devotional meringues for breakfast, or try to make beautiful fluffy omelettes full of fervor just when eggs are scarce. Dealing with her situation as it really is, and not proceeding on the assumption that it really ought to be something else, more interesting, exalted and flattering to self-love, she will be provident: not using up all her resources at the beginning of the week, or making plans she cannot carry out. She will refuse to translate the words "called to be saints" into "called to behave as if we were already saints." She will balance prayer and action, never giving out beyond her power, or forgetting to get in fresh supplies: so that her spiritual store cupboard is never bare. How mortified, free from all spiritual fancifulness and extravagance, is a life over which Prudence presides; love of God, even to contempt of self, determining all choices, purifying all motives, and maintaining an orderly, disciplined life in the soul....

Prudence further requires the careful handling of our own lives and capacities; instruments given us by God, and destined to be mirrors of His skill. It means choosing what helps, and rejecting what hinders, the fulfillment of that design, that vocation, which is already present in embryo in our souls....

•

Love chooses the work it can do, not the work that it likes. Prudent love took St. Thomas from contemplation, and made him the teacher of the schools. Prudent love does not insist on being a philanthropist when it lacks the warm outgoing temperament that is needed, and is decisively called to the more lonely but not less essential vocation of studying the deep things of God. It uses the material given it in the best possible way; and thus doing, makes its appointed contribution to that eternal plan which requires the perfect active surrender of the willing creature, the making of all choices and performance of all tasks in subservience to that God Who is Pure Act — the total consecration of natural life.

•

There are those who think first of their own spiritual hunger, and the imperative duty of feeding their own souls: those for whom the spiritual life means spiritual privilege — who defy common sense, take foolish risks, and call the proceeding trust in God: those who accept methods of recommending religion which are something less than spiritual, and call this "dealing with the conditions of modern life." All these courses in their different ways may seem prudent; and all wilt away before the selfless prudence of Christ....

The New Testament contains no single instance in which our Lord sought or obtained a private spiritual advantage: and the devout persons who do so are at best only vegetable-fiber saints. Like artificial silk, they look very glossy, but do not stand much wear and tear....

Love must learn by experience to recognize when the secret inward pressure comes from God, and when it really comes from self-will, and we persuade ourselves that it is the push of God. Nothing is more important than that we should faithfully follow our own true spiritual attraction; develop and use the talent given into our care. But it needs a humble and a prudent spirit to discover what that is, and distinguish it from the other more exciting kind of attraction which is really rooted in self-love....

How sober, mortified, truly discreet is the prayer of the saints; faithful, loyal, free from self-chosen peculiarities, keeping steadily on through darkness and through light....

It is one thing to make Love's choice, and quite another to stick to it. Nevertheless this is the right way to handle the ground floor life; not eliminating its frictions, but using its capacities, and gradually purifying the use of them from self-love. We can afford to have a warm and well-furnished kitchen, and even to take pride in it, so long as we remember that it is a kitchen; and that all its activities must be subservient to the interests of the whole house, and its observance of the city's law.

— The House of the Soul

WISE FURNISHINGS:
TEMPERANCE, MODERATION, FORTITUDE

If it is the special work of Prudence to manage our basement premises, so run the domestic life of the soul that all its willed choices, the trend of its behavior, subserve the purposes of God; it is the special work of Temperance to harness and control the natural instincts, and subdue them to the same end. Temperance, says St. Thomas, is the Virtue of the Beautiful, the virtue which tempers and orders our vehement desires, and subjects even our apparently spiritual cravings to the mortifying action of love: for moderation, proportion, reverence for conditions, is the very secret of a lasting beauty. To worship the Lord in the beauty of holiness does not mean the unbridled enthusiasm of the dervish, but the quiet and steadfast loyalty of the saint.

Temperance, then, must preside over the furnishing of the soul's house, if it is to be the setting of a useful, ordered, peaceful interior life. Much discipline, moderation, actual self-denial are involved in wise furnishing. No hurried purchase of the cheap or attractive, without considering the size and shape of our rooms; no copying of our neighbor's interesting new curtains, oblivious of the fact that they will never live with our dear old rugs; no frenzied efforts to get a grand piano into a two-roomed flat. If the house is to be a success, what we leave out will be quite as important as what we put in. *Abstine et sustine.* At every turn we are required to reconsider our first notions, accept our limitations, mortify our desires. . . .

So too we observe how moderate, humble, attuned to the scale of daily life are all the crucial events of the New Testament. Seen from the outside, none could have guessed their shattering and transfiguring power. . . . The quiet routine of a childhood and working life in Nazareth; the wandering ministry of teaching and compassion, with the least possible stress laid on supernatural powers; the homely little triumph of Palm Sunday; the pitiful sufferings of an arrest and execution too commonplace to disturb the city's life. . . .

In spite of its contrasts between the stern and tender, how steadily temperate and central in its emphasis is all His teaching: full of the color and quality of real life free from the merely startling, ever keeping close to our normal experience.

So too the restless energetic desire to get things done, the impetuous determination to remodel the world nearer to our hearts' desire, the exaggerated importance we attribute to our own action, the emphasis placed on doing, to the detriment of being — all this must be mortified if calm and order are to rule the lower floor.... Like Peter's wife's mother, while the fever is on us we cannot really serve our fellow men.

The paradox of peaceful striving runs right through the New Testament. Fortitude means the achievement, even on the natural level, of an inward stability which transcends the world of change. The small size of our premises matters little, if the walls are weather-proof and stand firm.

Such fortitude is not the virtue of the dashing soldier. It means rather the virtue of the keeper of the fortress; the inconspicuous heroism that sits tight. And in the life of the spirit there is a great deal of sitting tight; of refusing to be frightened out of it or decoyed away from it; of refusing to despair, waiting until the weather improves, till business gets brisker, day breaks, the shadows lift. We must endure a mysterious pressure, which operates more often and more purely in darkness than in light....

The peaceful, temperate, and balanced employment in God of those natural faculties and opportunities committed to us, choosing with self-oblivious love what helps, remembering that excess most often hinders, bearing and enduring all that the choice of His interests entails; this must bring order to our downstairs life, if the home is ever to be fit for its guest. "Peace," says St. Thomas Aquinas, "is the tranquillity of order; disquiet diminishes as sanctity increases." And if there is one characteristic which marks a genuine spiritual experience, that characteristic is surely the deep peace in which it places the soul. Thus a certain slowing down and spacing out of our ceaseless clockwork activities is a necessary condition of the deepening and enrichment of life. The spirit of Joy and the spirit of Hurry cannot live in the same house. But Joy, not Hurry, is an earnest of the Presence of God; an attribute of the creative life.

•

Without the steadying influences of Prudence, Temperance, and Fortitude, without the wise austerity of feeling, thought, and will which these require, who can hope to be quiet, and so prepare a habitation for that serene Spirit of Joy which is God? Without these, we are perpetually tormented by indecision, weakened by excesses, discouraged by failures; the trials and darkness which form part of the life of prayer defeat instead of bracing us, the very richness of experience and opportunity through which God molds our characters, bewilders us. It is not till the ground floor is in good order that we acquire the priceless art of doing one thing at a time, and doing it with total dedication, which is the foundation of an ordered life. The sense of cleavage between the duties of Mary and Martha, and a certain uneasy effort to combine them, is responsible for much psychic untidiness, tension, and weakening fuss. When the whole house is devoted to one interest, and a working harmony is established between the upper and the lower floor, each action, however homely, has the quality of prayer; since every corner and all that is done in it is informed by God and tends to God. It is the work of Prudence to discern and accept all that He proposes; because however odd it seems, it is the apt means of the soul's contact with Him. It is the work of Temperance to resist the temptation to bring in other things, crowd the soul's life with loves, labors, or devotions not truly proposed to it by God. It is the work of Fortitude to endure His molding action with tranquillity, and maintain our steadfast correspondence with His will. In the secret world of self-conquest, in all dealings with circumstance — people, opportunities, trials, tasks — and in the most hidden experiences of the spirit, it is on this triple foundation that the soul's deep action must rest. Here is the solid basis of that truly mortified and tranquil character which can bear the stress and burden of the supernatural life.

— *The House of the Soul*

WHEN CHARITY ENTERS

We have inspected both floors of the soul's house; stood in its watch tower, and studied its domestic arrangements — the disadvantages and possibilities of the double situation in which we are placed. Yet there still seems something lacking; something which must fill the whole house from basement to attic and bind in one both levels of life, if its upkeep is to be worth while, if it is to be anything more than a model dwelling without the atmosphere of a home. What is it that is wanting? Charity; the living Spirit of Creative Love. To be a home, a dwelling-place in time for that Spirit, the house has been swept and garnished, the best loved bits of rubbish have been sacrificed, the windows have been cleaned, the table set. It is not intended to be a showplace, but a real "habitation of God through the Spirit"; and the name of the Spirit is Charity. If Faith opened the eyes of the understanding on that threefold vision in which we see that only God is fully real; and if Hope so purified the mind's content that all dropped away but its trustful tendency to that unchanging Reality; then Charity transforms in God the very mainspring of character, the active will, and thus completes the spiritualization of man.

So Charity, when it enters the soul's house, swallows up and irradiates its Faith and Hope. "God *is* Charity," says St. John, "who dwells in Charity dwells in God."

•

Charity is no easy emotion. It does not merely consist in yielding to the unspeakable attraction of God. We are often terrified and always shamed, when we see what its achievement involved for the Saints; what steady endurance of darkness, what suffering and courage, are the price of their love, joy, and peace. The fire of Charity, lit in the soul, needs careful tending. The first tiny flame must not be allowed to die down for lack of fuel; and we may have to feed it with things we should prefer to keep for ourselves. It will only be developed and kept burning in a life informed by prayer — faithful, steady, mortified, self-oblivious prayer, the humble aspiration of the spirit to its Source: indeed, the very object of prayer is to increase and maintain Charity, the loving friendship of the soul with God.

All other aspects of the inner life are subsidiary to this and only of value in so far as they contribute to it. For the prayer of

Charity introduces us into the very atmosphere and presence of God, that secret chamber of the soul where He dwells; and shows us, obscurely but intensely, God as the one object of this soul's love and longing, and all struggles and sacrifices made in His interests as forms of joy. It lifts the heavy cloud of self-occupation from our spirits, transforms the mental and moral problems that torture us; they all look different in the light of that fire. "Love," says Thomas à Kempis, "sees causes of fear and feareth not; but as a quick brand or sparkle of fire flameth ever upward." And it is this constant desirous aspiration of the soul towards the Beloved Perfection, with its utter forgetfulness of personal dreads and risks, which delivers it from evil. "Adam sinned when he fell from contemplation" — and the essence of contemplation is the soul's loving attention to God. "Were we always simple," says Ruysbroeck, "and could we always contemplate with the same recollection, we should always have that same experience, which is our proper resting-place."

Within the prayer of Charity, too, we catch a glimpse of our own small life in the light of God, and of our own soul's house as it is meant to be — a habitation of the Creative Love. It is a bracing and a humbling vision. We see our vocation then, however prosaic, as a form of Charity; simply a call to express the creative love infused into us, in this or that way. For Charity introduces the soul into a vast organism, built of all striving, loving spirits; an organism which is destined to be possessed and used by God, for creative and redemptive work within the world.

Hence the only active works worth doing or worth having, are ultimately found to be those that proceed from Charity: that are the work of a soul adhering to God and acting as His tool.... A real act of Charity is the exact opposite of an act of philanthropy. It is done wholly to, for, and in God; for His sake, as a contribution to His purpose, because we see the situation from His point of view....

Thus in the last resort Christian perfection, in fact the whole course of the spiritual life, is found to be the same thing as Charity — the loving union of the human spirit with the Eternal Spirit

of God. Nothing but this love will drive it to the heroic struggles, self-stripping, and purifications, maintain it through the long
slow climb with many humbling falls, whereby it is remade in
the image of the Absolute Love. The soul that plays for safety,
even spiritual safety, never becomes perfect. "Real Charity," says
St. John of the Cross, "is not shown merely by tender feelings,
but by a strength, courage, and endurance unknown to other
souls." The true lover, wholly given to God and His interests, is
released from all carefulness about his own interests, safety, and
comfort. Thus not Faith and Hope alone, but Prudence, Temperance, and Fortitude too, are found in the last resort to be
swallowed up in Charity....

•

The Cross is the supreme symbol of that double movement of
Charity; the pouring forth of self-oblivious love, up towards God,
outwards towards men, and surely downwards too, to all the
smaller children of God. Here we are confronted by a Charity
as rich, wide, and deep as Creation, entirely self-giving and entirely undemanding, which loves God first, its fellows next, itself
not at all; the consummation of a life in which prayer and work,
teaching and healing, joy and suffering, were simply the different
strings of an instrument on which was played the only music of
the Love of God. And in those Saints who approach their model
most nearly, as did St. Francis, this widespreading love is the very
substance of perfection, and ultimate source of their life-giving
power. They are complete in their self-giving, like God. "Because," says Ruysbroeck, "the living fountain of the Holy Spirit,
which is their wealth, can never be spent," they are become dis-
tributors of His creative and redeeming energy. Their passionate
identification with His interests flows out in an endless variety
of expression to share His love and care for other men: and it is
this, more than any moral correctness, any exemption from special faults or failings, which is the earnest of their supernatural
life....

Faith may release the mind from the tyranny of the here-and-now, and Hope may seem to concentrate the whole drive of our being upon the Reality of God. Only Charity can thus weave together both worlds, both levels of the soul's life; and, making our love of God and of His creatures one, provides a habitation, a gathering point for the Creative Love, and opens a channel through which it can be applied to each detail of His unfinished world. Thus it is, as the mystics say, that Charity makes God and the soul "one thing." Some of the difficulties surrounding the life of prayer, and particularly of intercession, might vanish, did we understand it as an application to particular cases of the boundless Charity of God; an application which is effected by means of our will and love....

Charity puts us in line with all the noblest aspects of Creation — the generous outpouring of sunshine, the uncalculating fertility of the earth, the great life-giving mantle of air; all those undemanding gifts which condition our existence, and are reflected fragments of that unlimited self-giving which is the fundamental character of God.

The New Testament is full of reminders of the transcendent worth, the life-giving quality, of this generous unlimited love: the love that pours out the precious ointment, and then breaks the vase and gives that too; that throws in the second mite after the first; that sets aside as equally irrelevant personal desires, personal failings, and personal achievements. The Charity willing to feed the sheep and lambs, and go on and on chopping the turnips and tending the fold, for the sake of the Beloved: adoration and penitence blossoming in homely service....

•

The House of the Soul, then, must be an open house for all who are sent to it; all for whom there are things to be done; all who are proposed to its fostering care. Its welcome must be as wide as that Poverty which, empty of itself, has room for all. Upstairs and downstairs, in work and in prayer, it must wholly serve

the creative purpose; mortifying the desire of devotional sweetness, ignoring the claims of spiritual comfort, and bringing all
the needs of the city, and of the vast desolate world beyond the
city, within the area of its widespreading love....

"When the evening of this life comes," says St. John of the
Cross, "you will be judged on love." The only question asked
about the soul's use of its two-storied house and the gifts that
were made to it, will be: "Have you loved well?" All else will
be resumed in this; all thoughts, beliefs, desires, struggles, and
achievements, all the complex activities of the upper and lower
floor. For Faith is nothing unless it be the obscure vision of a
loved Reality; and Hope is nothing, unless it be the confidence
of perfect love. So too with all the persons, events, opportunities, conflicts, and choices proposed for the soul's purification
and growth. Was everything that was done, done for love's sake?
Were all the doors opened, that the warmth of Charity might
fill the whole house; the windows cleaned, that they might more
and more radiate from within its mysterious divine light? Is the
separate life of the house more and more merged in the mighty
current of the city's life? Is it more and more adapted to the city's
sacred purpose — the saving radiation of the Perfect within an
imperfect world? For this is Charity; the immense expansion of
personality effected by the love of God, weaving together the natural and the supernatural powers of the soul, and filling them
with its abundant life. Overflowing the barriers of preference,
passing through all contrary appearance, it mediates the Divine
pity and generosity to every mesh and corner of creation; and
rests at last in God, Who is the life and lover of every soul.

— The House of the Soul

3

Aspects of Mysticism

Part of Underhill's task is to convince her readers that mysticism is firmly rooted in the Judeo-Christian tradition. While such an idea may seem commonplace today, Underhill was working against a perception of mysticism as belonging to faraway religions and foreign shores. In the following selections from Mystics of the Church, *Underhill gives us a mysticism that is as close to us as the Bible. She insists that mysticism belongs to the Hebrew, the Catholic, and the Protestant traditions.*

MYSTICISM IN THE BIBLE:
ST. PAUL

Christian literature begins with a handful of letters written by a mystic: that is to say, with the epistles of St. Paul, the oldest books of the New Testament. Though we might well appeal to the Synoptic portrait of Jesus, as our real guarantee for that balanced life of loving communion with God and active charity to men which is the ideal of Christian mysticism — still, the Gospels as we have them are later than St. Paul's career. This means that the earliest documentary witness to Jesus Christ which we possess is the witness of mysticism; and it tells us, not about His earthly life, but about the intense and transfiguring experience of His continued presence, enjoyed by one who had never known

Him in the flesh. With St. Paul all that is most distinctive of truly Christian mysticism bursts on the world in its richest form, becomes the inspiration of his missionary labors, and is bequeathed by him to the infant community. Therefore any account of the office which the mystics fill in the church must begin here.

Yet even at this apparent fountain-head the solidarity of mankind, the dependence of the soul, not only on God but also on other souls, shows itself. Christian mysticism has its roots in pre-Christian history. The voice which spoke to St. Paul on the road to Damascus addressed a mind steeped in the Old Testament, colored especially by its prophetic writings, and accepting without question the prophetic claim to a first-hand experience of God. If, then, by the mysticism of the New Testament we must chiefly understand the claim of the first disciples to direct communion with the Spirit of Jesus, that mysticism contains and hands on factors already present in the highest forms of Jewish religion. It was fed by Hebrew literature, perhaps specially by the Psalms; and the Church, basing on those psalms her own devotional life, was true to a great historic fact. Though on its philosophic side later Christian mysticism is often said to be derived from the Neoplatonists, this dependence on Scripture is its real characteristic. From St. Augustine to Blake, all its great figures are emphatically "Bible Christians"; and obscure Biblical phrases are the real sources of many of those symbols and images over which students now puzzle and dispute.

A conviction of direct communion with God — a vivid consciousness of His reality and presence — is characteristic of all the loftiest Old Testament writers, and indeed of Jewish personal religion as a whole....

In such a verse as 1 Kings 19:12 we surely recognize that absolute certitude which comes into the mind of the mystic through the deep quiet of his contemplation. Such experiences were the true, indeed the only possible, source of the immense demand for a genuine and not merely formal purity and righteousness which these men and their successors made on the still half-civilized Hebrew tribes of their day....

In the earliest stages of Hebrew prophecy, as in other primitive religions, ecstasy — supposed to involve Divine possession, but most often releasing subconscious intuitions and dreams of varying degrees of value — seems to have been deliberately induced, by music, dancing, and other devices....

But, once we acknowledge the unity of man's religious sense, we see that the reluctant Jeremiah accepting his destiny from the inward monitions of God, or Isaiah going three years barefoot and dressed as a captive at the Divine command, are the true spiritual ancestors of the apostle "who was not disobedient to the heavenly vision," and in the strength which that vision gave him created the Gentile Church....

St. Paul, then, the first and one of the greatest of the Church's mystics, looking forward to the great procession of Christian mystical saints and giving them the language in which their most sacred apprehensions were to be expressed, looks back to the Hebrew prophets and psalmists, and testifies to the unbroken stream of spiritual life which quickens the Church. We recognize easily in him the three-fold strand of the "mystic way": the moral struggles and purifications, so vividly described in Romans; the deep insights and illuminations characteristic of the developing life of prayer; the sense of unbroken union with Christ which sustained his immense activities; the final achievement of that surrender and rebirth in power by which he was able to say, "I live, yet not I."

•

The reaction to God or to Christ of the real mystical temperament, once it is awakened, is always what psychology calls an all-or-none reaction. The whole impulsive nature first resists, and then, when at last the pressure becomes too strong, capitulates completely.

Of this law the conversion of St. Paul provides a perfect illustration. His initiation into the mystical life was both realistic and ecstatic in character....

The violent breaking up of his resistances, the flooding of his mind with a new loyalty and love, produced in this ardent temperament intense psycho-physical effects. The impression of a dazzling light was followed by a brief functional blindness, in which he remained three days without food or drink; marking the intensity of the crisis in which he had passed from the old to the new life....

The fact which mainly concerns us is this: in his mystical experience he breaks entirely new ground. He is the unique link between the primitive apostolic experiences of communion with the Risen Jesus and the still-continued Christocentric mysticism of the Church; and might with some justice be called both the first of Evangelicals and first of Catholics.

If, then, we are to obtain a true idea of St. Paul's personality and the source of his amazing powers, we must correct the view which sees him mainly as theologian and organizer by that which recognizes in him a great contemplative.

•

Ecstatic phenomena were almost taken for granted in the Early Church; and St. Paul's distinction as a mystic lies not in their possession, but in the detachment with which he regarded them. Thus in A.D. 52, when he wrote his first letter to the Corinthians, he acknowledged his continued possession of the much-prized "gift of tongues"; those outbursts of ecstatic but unintelligible speech common in times of religious excitement. But his attitude toward such external "manifestations of the Spirit" is marked by a cool common sense which must amaze us when we consider the period in which he wrote, the universal respect for the marvelous, and the circumstances of his own conversion. His rule is simple. He discounts any "gifts" and experiences which do not help other souls. The mystical communion of his soul with Christ must not be a matter of personal enjoyment; it must support and not supplant the apostolic career. "Forasmuch as ye are zealous of spiritual gifts, seek that ye may excel to the upbuilding of the

Church.... I will pray with the Spirit, *and* I will pray with the understanding too."

•

We can trace a distinct progress from the stress and vehemence of St. Paul's earlier writings to that tranquil joy and peace which mark real maturity of soul, and are the outstanding characteristics of Philippians. His mystical conceptions are already developed in the period of 1 Corinthians, with its great distinction between the "psychic" or intellectual, and the spiritually sensitive man, and its declaration of the hidden wisdom revealed by the immanent spirit "that searcheth *all* things; yea, the *deep* things of God," to those who have the mind of Christ (1 Cor. 2:10).

We notice in Romans, the typical letter of his middle period, (c. A.D. 56), a growing sense of power, stability, and freedom; a condition closely associated in St. Paul's mind with the idea of "Grace." "Grace" is for him no theological abstraction, but an actual, inflowing energy, which makes possible man's transition from the natural to the supernatural state.

Anyone who still supposes him to be predominantly a legalist should consider how profoundly supernatural a conception of Christianity underlies the opening paragraph of Romans; what a struggle to describe the actual but subtle facts of the inner life is to be felt in its greatest passages, which often seek to suggest an experience beyond the range of common speech. This letter is the work of a man who has fully emerged into a new sphere of consciousness, has been "made free by the Spirit of Life," "a new creature," and enjoys that sense of boundless possibility which he calls "the glorious liberty of the children of God" (8:21). He knows the mysterious truth, which only direct experience can bring home to us, that somehow even in this determined world "*all* things work together for good to them that love God." Nor does he fail to link this grand, because selfless, confidence with the tensions and sufferings of the practical life. "Who shall separate us from the love of Christ? Shall tribulation, or distress, or

persecution, or famine, or nakedness, or peril, or sword? ... Nay, in all these things we are more than conquerors" (8:35, 37).
— *Mystics of the Church*

FRANCISCAN MYSTICISM

With the career of St. Francis of Assisi (1182–1226) something new entered the spiritual life of the church ... a mysticism which was penitential, uncloistered, poetic, and Christlike. Since in varying degrees these qualities reappeared in the spiritual experience of his followers, enriching through them the Christian consciousness, Francis must rank with those creative personalities to whom all the deepest developments of this consciousness are due....

A real return to the Gospels is always startling, whatever the circumstances in which it takes place. The return made by St. Francis seemed to his contemporaries so amazing in its novelty, vigor, and completeness, and in the transformation it effected, that he came to be regarded by his disciples and their immediate successors as, above all, the perfect imitator of Christ: one, indeed, in whom the actual earthly life of Jesus was reproduced. "Christ hath shown Himself in thee!" said Jacopone da Todi with his usual boldness.

More attractive is the form taken by this conception in the beautiful mind of Pier Pettignano (d. 1289), that humble Franciscan contemplative whom all readers of Dante love. He saw in vision a superb procession of Apostles, Saints, and Martyrs, with the Blessed Virgin at their head; all walking carefully and scrutinizing the ground with much earnestness, that they might tread as nearly as possible in the very footsteps of Christ. At the end of this pageant of the Church Triumphant came the little shabby figure of Francis, barefoot and brown-robed; and he alone was walking easily and steadily in the actual footprints of our Lord. Such tales as these show what the life and rule of Francis meant to those who were touched by his spirit; and give the starting-point of Franciscan mysticism, with its love of poetry and vivid Christocentric feeling.

The peculiar concentration on the Passion which unites all the Franciscan mystics, of course results from the episode of the stigmata, which deeply impressed the medieval religious mind. Whatever be our opinion of this episode, it witnesses to the intense and mystical character of that inner life which St. Francis — like his Pattern [i.e., Jesus Christ] — so well concealed from the outer world. As the Gospels tell almost nothing about the interior education that ended in Gethsemane; so the gradual development of the spirit of Francis during the eighteen years of his religious life can only be judged by its culmination on La Verna, when, for an instant, the body became completely docile to the longings and apprehensions of the soul.

All the great Franciscan mystics, differing widely in temperament from each other and from Francis himself, live under the spell of this event. It gives them the passionate enthusiasm for suffering on the one hand, the rapturous and almost lyrical joy in surrender on the other, with which they enriched the consciousness of the Church. This ecstasy of self-giving, this paradoxical union of painful and delighted love, is not, of course, chiefly to be sought within the respectable ranks of those "conventual" friars who learnt so soon to interpret the Rule of Poverty in accordance with comfort and common sense. It was preserved and handed on by the saintly brothers who kept intact the spirit of St. Francis; men living chiefly in remote hermitages, where they observed the Primitive Rule in all its rigor and passed their time in prayer....

These humble servants of the supernatural were known, revered, and visited in their retreats by all who valued the life of the Spirit; and thus preserved and disseminated in its ardor and purity the inner character of Franciscan mysticism.

Second only to their influence was the part played by the Franciscan Tertiaries. These were men and women of all ranks, living in the world, who were drawn by the unmatched attraction of the Franciscan appeal and demand to accept such a modified rule of simplicity and devotion as was consistent with ordinary life; and formed a loosely-knit society devoted to spiritual religion. It was within this society that the great Franciscan mystics — Pier Pettignano, Jacopone da Todi, Angela of Foligno, and Ubertino de Casale — developed.

•

Angela is an admirable example of that which the Abbé Huvelin was accustomed to call a "bit by bit spirituality." Even allowing for the exaggeration of the penitent, she had clearly lived, until the beginning of middle age, a thoroughly worldly and even a sinful life; yet she became one of the great religious influences of her day, and was called, not without reason, a "Mistress in Theology." Her best known disciple, Ubertino de Casale, has left an impressive picture of her spiritual power; and that which he experienced we may be sure that many others experienced too.

Ubertino was a vain, brilliant and self-indulgent young friar, whose first initiation into the spiritual life, at the hands of Cecilia of Florence and Pier Pettignano, had merely stimulated his religious imagination and stopped short of real self-renouncement. He preached brilliantly but lived comfortably; and his complete conversion was only effected when he came under the influence of Angela at about forty years of age, and received through her direction the strength of purpose he required. "She restored, even a thousand-fold, all the gifts of my soul that I had lost through my sinfulness, so that from henceforth I was not the same man as before..." (*Arbor Vitae,* Prologue).

The woman of whom this is written, at that time about fifty years old, had passed through a long apprenticeship and much interior suffering before reaching the creative levels of spiritual life.

She had, like most of the great mystics, strong natural passions, and endured prolonged struggle in the course of their sublimation and dedication to spiritual ends. A married woman in prosperous circumstances, she loved human life, with its luxuries and comforts; was sensual, self-indulgent, vacillating and insincere; and first combined full enjoyment of the world with the pretended practice of Franciscan austerity. "Being the while full of greediness, gluttony, and drunkenness, I feigned to desire naught, save what was needful . . . " (*Book of Conversion,* cap. 1). This picture is not attractive; seldom, indeed, has more un-promising material been used for the making of a saint.

Angela was probably at this time a nominal Franciscan Ter-tiary, evading the real obligations of the Rule. Furthermore she had committed grave sins which she was afraid to confess, until, praying to St. Francis, he appeared to her in a dream, and prom-ised her help. Going next day to the cathedral of Foligno, she saw in the pulpit her uncle Arnaldo, a Franciscan friar, and recogniz-ing in him the promised helper, made her confession to him thus taking the first of the "spiritual steps" by which she "came to know the imperfections of her life," and sought to correct then. This process lasted for years.

•

It was when she decided upon full renunciation of property that Angela first knew the joys as well as the compulsions of the spir-itual life. Hitherto she had been "sunk in bitterness because of her sins, and feeling no divine sweetness whatsoever." But after she had resolved on perfect poverty, she was given "so clear an understanding of the divine goodness and mine own unworthi-ness that I could in no way describe it," and from this time began to "feel the sweetness and consolation of God in her heart."

The state of illumination was completed and her consecration assured by the most celebrated of her spiritual "revelations": the experience which befell her as she went on a pilgrimage from Foligno to Assisi. She tells us that a little time before, whilst she was still distributing the remainder of her property to the poor, she had said to God in prayer, "Lord, that which I do, I do only that I may find Thee," and it seemed to her that a voice replied, "Strive diligently to make thyself ready, for when thou hast ac-complished that which thou art now doing, the whole Trinity will descend unto thee." The most ancient manuscript of Angela's revelations tells us that it was precisely when she came to the little chapel of the Holy Trinity, where the road from Spello turns toward Assisi, that she suddenly felt her soul inundated by the Presence of God, who spoke to her and "persuaded her to love," promising to remain with her till her second visit to the basilica of Assisi.

•

Arnaldo wrote at her dictation the unequaled series of "intellectual visions" which give her a special place among the mystics of the Church.... Though Angela frequently complained of their inadequacy, insisting that his words were "dry and savorless" and hardly suggested the ineffable truths which were revealed to her, this record remains one of the greatest monuments of Christian mysticism. "The eyes of my soul were opened, and I beheld the plenitude of God, whereby I did comprehend the whole world, both here and beyond the sea, and the abyss and all things else.... Wherefore I did now comprehend that the world is but a small thing; I saw, moreover, that the power of God was above all things, and that the whole world was filled with it."

•

For Angela, the beginning and end of true wisdom was "to know God and ourselves" — a level of reality which few human beings achieve.... "Every vision, every revelation, all sweetness and emotion, all knowledge, all contemplation, availeth nothing if a man know not God and himself!" This realistic knowledge, this sense of spiritual proportion, depends on the soul's humility and poverty. In true Franciscan fashion, she identifies this lowliness and emptiness of spirit with that literal imitation of the earthly life of Christ to which every awakened soul is bound. "The love of God," she observes in a celebrated passage, "is never idle, for it constrains us to follow the way of the Cross!...For as we know, so do we love; therefore if we know but little and darkly, if we reflect and meditate on Him only superficially and fleetingly, we shall in consequence love Him but little." Real love is to be directed with discretion, and shown in the acceptance of hardship and contempt, the practice of humility, gentleness, and steadfastness — a catalogue of virtues which perhaps reflects the course followed by Angela's own interior transformation. And the end of this hard process is declared to be the revelation that "*all* goodness cometh from the Love Uncreate, and not from ourselves — whosoever feeleth this hath the Spirit of Truth!"

"Thou," said Jacopone da Todi more tersely, "art the Love wherewith the heart loves Thee." In these two sayings, so deceptive in their simplicity, so infinite in their scope, we reach the heart of Franciscan mysticism.   — *Mystics of the Church*

SOME PROTESTANT MYSTICS

There had grown up in all parts of England groups of spiritual "seekers" or "waiters" — a term first applied to them in 1617. Distinguished on the one hand by a strong tendency to Quietism, on the other by belief in individual illumination...these — as William Penn afterwards said of them — "left all visible churches and societies and wandered up and down as sheep without a shepherd...*seeking* their Beloved, but could not find Him as their souls desired to know Him." Influenced by the mystical and quietist literature which was now in general circulation, some practiced great austerity of life and met regularly for silent prayer. Their importance in the history of the Church consists in the fact that they provided the spiritual landscape within which the mystical genius of George Fox (1624–91) developed; and that the formation of the Society of Friends, that great experiment in corporate mysticism, largely represents their discovery, under his leadership, of the treasure they had sought....

The Quaker method...witnesses to the mighty results that may be achieved by an uncompromising Christian inwardness; and shows how simple men and women may share the essential experiences of the contemplative life, and reach a first-hand appreciation of God inciting to heroic action and rivaling the

conclusions of mystical philosophers. All this is ultimately derived from the spiritual creativeness of Fox himself, one of those
great and life-giving personalities through whom from time to
time the Spirit reaches out to men.

Fox, born of the craftsman class, and brought up in a strict
but arid Puritan atmosphere, which could not satisfy his innate
craving for spiritual reality, felt in adolescence the inward turmoil
and longing for assurance so characteristic of religious genius of
the "twice-born" type. At nineteen he left home and became in
body as well as soul a "seeker." ... "I was," he says, "a man of
sorrows in the time of the first workings of the Lord in me. This
period of conflict lasted for three years." It was brought to an
end by the great and well-known ecstatic experience, compara-
ble to those in which St. Augustine and St. Francis were born
into new life, which gave him, once for all, absolute certitude.
"Then, O then, I heard a Voice which said, 'There is one, even
Christ Jesus, that can speak to thy condition'; and when I heard
it, my heart did leap for joy...." In view of Fox's subsequent
career, we cannot doubt that this is the description of a genuine mystical conversion, an opening of "the eye which looks
on eternity." It was indeed the first of those openings, or abrupt
ecstatic apprehensions, which witness to his abnormal psychic
constitution and supported his apostolic life. It was probably in
the following year that the establishment of his consciousness on
these new levels was completed in a prolonged trance — said to
have lasted fourteen days — during which his whole bodily aspect became changed; and he afterwards declared that he had
been through "a very ocean of darkness and death" into "the
greatness and infinitude of the Love of God which cannot be
expressed in words... an infinite ocean of light and love which
flowed over the ocean of darkness." These phrases inevitably remind us of [Jacob] Boehme, whose works were eagerly devoured
by the early Quakers and must have been known to Fox by the
time his *Journal* was composed; and there are other "openings"
which approach even more closely in character to Boehme's great
pictorial intuitions of reality: "All things were new; and all the

creation gave another smell unto me than before, beyond what words can utter.... The creation was opened to me; and it was showed me how all things had their names given them, according to their nature and virtue."

Such passages, all belonging to his first period of growth, prove Fox to have been a visionary; but it is the apostolic life which developed from and through these experiences which gives him an honored place among the mystics of the Church. In a period of arid religious formalism he brought back, because he possessed it, the life-giving sense of the Presence of God.... Fox's ecstatic openings prepared him for a wandering ministry which lasted forty years, often involved persecution, hardship, and danger, and included visits to Holland, Germany, and Bermuda, and two years in America.... Uniting spiritual power with that stern common sense and capacity for detail so often found in the saints, he organized his groups with the thoroughness and success of a new St. Paul, coloring them with his own peculiar spirit and infecting them with his enthusiastic energy.... With little education, and often rough and intolerant in manner, he is, nevertheless, an outstanding example of the "power of the Spirit"; and there is much contemporary evidence of the immense impression which was made by his transfigured personality. Said William Penn of him: "The most awful, living, reverent frame I ever felt or beheld was his in prayer." An equivalent witness to that which would now be called his "numinous" quality came from the Cambridge students who had assembled to attack him, but exclaimed, "O hee shines, hee glisters!" and let him go unharmed — a story which should be compared with the insistent and unexplained reports of abnormal radiance which meet us in the lives of earlier mystics.

•

Yet it is impossible to read the first-hand accounts of Quaker faith and life, based wholly on the principle of loving surrender and the "practice of the Presence of God," without perceiving the close identity between their fundamental ideas and those of the great saints of contemporary France. At many points the Quaker and the Catholic contemplative approach one another. It is significant that Quaker spirituality of the second generation was nourished, not only by the writings of Boehme and his precursors and followers, but also by the great masters of traditional mysticism, especially Thomas à Kempis and Fénelon. In these the Friends found these very principles that governed their own religious practice; and through them they are linked with the great historic current of Christian spirituality.

These writers fed the loving and courageous soul of John Woolman (1720–72); whose deep mystical consciousness of the unity in love of God and man drove him to vigorous and unpopular denunciations of slavery, and beyond this to a "concern" for the animal creation Franciscan in its tenderness and unique in his period and place. "I was early convinced" (he says in his *Journal*) "that true religion consisted in an inward life, wherein the Heart doth Love and Reverence God the Creator, and learn to exercise true Justice and Goodness, not only toward all men, but also toward the Brute Creatures. . . . "

As Woolman's soul matured, his self-abandonment and austerities increased. Like Fox, he felt the call to take on himself the sorrows of the world.

•

The light of true Quaker spirituality, at once so inward and so active, passed from Woolman to a succession of saintly and vigorous souls. It is seen again in Stephen Grellet (1773–1855), that untiring missionary of the Inward Light, and in the heroic prison-reformer Elizabeth Fry (1780–1845), who found in the silence that mysterious power which "loves the unlovely into loveableness." These convince us of the continuously life-giving character of that Spirit which George Fox served and proclaimed.

Though the influence of Jacob Boehme is most marked in the Quakers, and other sectarian promoters of religious inwardness, and later in the quite unchurched mysticism of [William] Blake (1757–1827), that powerful genius also contributed something to the revival of mysticism in the Anglican Church. Through the interpretations of his great disciple William Law (1686–1761) his teachings brought their renewing touch to English institutionalism at one of the most deadly moments of its career. William Law's few mystical writings were produced in the later part of his life; for Boehme's influence reached him in middle age....

We cannot doubt that he experienced that interior transformation which he passionately proclaims; and which turned the brilliant ecclesiastic into the gentle and saintly recluse and director of souls, who wrote *The Spirit of Love* and *The Spirit of Prayer*. Through these little books, into which Law poured the fruits of his deep musings and his secret communion with God, he has influenced, and continues to influence, many souls.

•

Since the Evangelical Revival was mainly a return to religious realism, and especially to that ardent personal devotion which has always formed one strand in the Church's secret life, we might expect to find in it a nursery of mystics. This, notoriously, it did not become. Nevertheless, in the greatest souls whom it nourished, we see again the special quality of sanctity, tender, childlike, heroic, and contagious, which is the characteristic product of Christocentric mysticism. In Henry Martyn (1781–1812) we have a typical and beautiful example of its transforming power. A study of this half-forgotten scholar-mystic, who, in an atmosphere even hostile to the ideals of Catholicism, was possessed of the same experience, and driven to the same disciplines, as the mystics of the medieval Church, may well complete our survey of Protestant mysticism. Here we may realize its substantial identity with the classic Christian expressions of spiritual life.

Born at Truro, and growing up in a religious atmosphere colored by Wesley's influence, Martyn was a brilliant, hypersensitive, unstable, not specially religious boy. His conversion took place at Cambridge, and was chiefly due to the influence of Charles

Simeon. Simeon, a generation older than Martyn — mystical, passionately Christocentric, full of energy, courting persecution for the sake of his ideals — was one of the great apostolic souls of the Evangelical movement. Martyn, though a Wesleyan background and the immense impression made upon him by the life of David Brainerd counted for much in his development, is essentially his spiritual child. . . .

At twenty-one he was Senior Wrangler, and assured of a brilliant academic career. Two years later he was ordained, and under the dominion of his growing desire to help and redeem, was struggling as one of Charles Simeon's curates. . . . He had now begun, too, that impassioned study of Oriental languages in which, for the rest of his life, he found interest and refreshment. . . . In 1805 . . . he sailed for India as a missionary chaplain. Only the spiritual journal kept during these years reveals his true life, and the springs of action which dictated his sacrifices. . . .

During the physical hardships and intense spiritual loneliness of the nine months' journey to India, in pastoral charge of a ship's company of the roughest type, a manifest deepening of his mystical life took place. . . .

Thus the man who reached Calcutta in 1806 had already achieved something like spiritual maturity: a fact soon recognized by those capable of appreciating it. . . . "I wish," said Martyn, "to have my whole soul swallowed up in the Will of God"; and we seem to see the fulfillment of this desire through the reports of his contemporaries. "The outbeaming of his soul," said one who knew him, "would absorb the attention of every observer"; and another, "he shines in all the dignity of love, and seems to carry about him such a heavenly majesty, as impresses the mind beyond description."

. . . He could turn from the uphill pastoral labors of an Anglo-Indian chaplain of that day to his great and absorbing work of translating the New Testament into Hindustani, Arabic, and Persian — a task in which nothing satisfied him which fell below the level of the most exact scholarship — and from this again to delighted intercourse with the children or animals by whom he was always adored....

•

The last years of Martyn's short and various life have a heroic and romantic character which link him with such missionary mystics as St. Francis Xavier, whom he so greatly admired and envied, and the intrepid saint of the Sahara, Charles de Foucauld.

Driven by ill-health from India, he could not rest, but traveled with much difficulty to Persia, that he might get his translation of the Scriptures revised by Persian scholars. We have in his letters a vivid and amazing picture of his life in Shiraz; the gentle, studious, and fragile Evangelical clergyman, now disguised in Persian dress and adopting local manners, "but still singing hymns over my milk and water," since "tea I have none." Alone amongst a hostile Moslem population, to whom he fearlessly preached the Christian faith, he was yet "clothed in an almost magical calm"; and was recognized by the more spiritual among them as belonging to the universal company of the saints. Deep conversations took place between the Christian missionary and the Sufi mystics, whom he quaintly described as "the Methodists of the East."

"I am sometimes led on," he said, "to tell them all I know of the very recesses of the sanctuary; and these are the things that interest them." The "love clear, sweet, and strong" which glorified and supported Martyn's sufferings and efforts here transcended creedal barriers, and revealed one to another these diverse seekers for an identical Reality. His task finished, he started for England in a dying condition; and after a journey marked by the extremes of physical misery and spiritual joy died in great loneliness at Tokat, aged only thirty-one. — *Mystics of the Church*

4

The Soul's Journey

Underhill's groundbreaking study Mysticism *describes and documents many stages of the classical mystical path. Her discussion relies on a long tradition of mystical writers from many centuries. Nine of the following selections are taken from* Mysticism. *In a number of these passages, Underhill is dealing with the more difficult or troubling aspects of mystical life, such as the experience of darkness in prayer. Yet, even when she is in her most scholarly mode, there is a certain simple practicality about her explanations. The tenth selection, "Glorified," is from* The School of Charity, *a book of meditations on the Christian creed. It provides a fine summary of the "journey's end."*

THE CHARACTERISTICS
OF MYSTICISM

I think that we have already reached a point at which William James's celebrated "four marks" of the mystic state, Ineffability, Noetic Quality, Transiency, and Passivity (*Varieties of Religious Experience*), will fail to satisfy us. In their place I propose to set out, illustrate, and, I hope, justify four other rules or notes which may be applied as tests to any given case which claims to take its rank among the mystics.

1. True mysticism is active and practical, not passive and theoretical. It is an organic life-process, something which the whole self does; not something as to which its intellect holds an opinion.

2. Its aims are wholly transcendental and spiritual. It is in no way concerned with adding to, exploring, rearranging, or improving anything in the visible universe. The mystic brushes aside that universe, even in its supernormal manifestations. Though he does not, as his enemies declare, neglect his duty to the many, his heart is always set upon the changeless One.

3. This One is for the mystic, not merely the Reality of all that is, but a living and personal Object of Love; never an object of exploration. It draws his whole being homeward, but always under the guidance of the heart.

4. Living union with this One — which is the term of his adventure — is a definite state or form of enhanced life....It is arrived at by an arduous psychological and spiritual process — the so-called Mystic Way — entailing the complete remaking of character and the liberation of a new, or rather latent, form of consciousness....

Mysticism, then, is not an opinion: it is not a philosophy.... It is the name of the organic process which involves the perfect consummation of the Love of God: the achievement here and now of the immortal heritage of man. Or if you like it better — for this means exactly the same thing — it is the art of establishing his conscious relation with the Absolute....

"Whether we live or whether we die," said St. Paul, "we are the Lord's." The mystic is a realist, to whom these words convey not a dogma but an invitation: an invitation to the soul to attain that fullness of life for which she was made, to "lose herself in That which can be neither seen nor touched...." Mysticism, then, is seen as the "one way out" for the awakened spirit of man; healing that human incompleteness which is the origin of our divine unrest. "I am sure," says Eckhart, "that if a soul knew the least of all that Being means, it would never turn away from it." The mystics have never turned away: to do so would have seemed to them a self-destructive act. There, in this world of illusion, they say, we have no continuing city....

To sum up. Mysticism is seen to be a highly specialized form of that search for reality, for heightened and completed life, which we have found to be a constant characteristic of human consciousness.... So strange and exalted is this life that it never fails to provoke the anger or the admiration of other men.

— Mysticism

THE AWAKENING OF THE SELF

Now, the opening of St. Francis's eyes, which took place in A.D. 1206 when he was twenty-four years old, had been preceded by a long, hard struggle between the life of the world and the persistent call of the spirit. His mind, in modern language, had not unified itself. He was a high-spirited boy, full of vitality: a natural artist, with all the fastidiousness which the artistic temperament involves. War and pleasure both attracted him, and upon them, says his legend, he "miserably squandered and wasted his time" (Thomas of Celano, *Legenda Prima,* cap. i). Nevertheless, he was vaguely dissatisfied. In the midst of festivities, he would have sudden fits of abstraction.... He loved beauty, for he was by nature a poet and musician, but shrank instinctively from contact with ugliness and disease. But something within ran counter to this temperamental bias, and sometimes conquered it. He would then associate with beggars, tend the leprous, perform impulsive acts of charity and self-humiliation.

When this divided state, described by the legend as "the attempt to flee God's hand," had lasted for some years, it happened one day that he was walking in the country outside the gates of Assisi, and passed the little church of S. Damiano.... "And, being led by the Spirit, he went in to pray; and he fell down before the Crucifix in devout supplication, and *having been smitten by unwonted visitations, found himself another man than he who had gone in*" (Thomas of Celano, *Legenda Secunda,* cap. v).

Here, then, is the first stage of conversion. The struggle between two discrepant ideals of life has attained its term. A sudden and apparently "irrational" impulse to some decisive act reaches the surface-consciousness from the seething depths. The impulse is followed; and the swift emergence of the transcendental sense results. This "unwonted visitation" effects an abrupt and involuntary alteration in the subject's consciousness: whereby he literally finds himself another man. He is as one who has slept and now awakes....

In many conversions to the mystic life, the revelation of an external splendor, the shining vision of the transcendent spiritual world, is wholly absent. The self awakes to that which is within, rather than to that which is without: to the immanent not the transcendent God, to the personal not the cosmic relation....

A never to be ended give-and-take is set up between the individual and the Absolute. The Spirit of Life has been born: and the first word it learns to say is *Abba,* Father.... So, even at its very beginning, we see how active, how profoundly organic, how deeply and widely alive is the true contemplative life.... The awakening of the self is to a new and more active plane of being, new and more personal relations with Reality; hence to a new and more real work which it must do.   — *Mysticism*

THE PURIFICATION OF THE SELF

To the true lover of the Absolute, Purgation no less than Illumination is a privilege, a dreadful joy. It is an earnest of increasing life. "Let me suffer or die!" said St. Teresa: a strange alternative in the ears of common sense, but a forced option in the spiritual sphere. However harsh its form, however painful the activities to which it spurs him, the mystic recognizes in this breakup of his old universe an essential part of the Great Work.... "Teach me, my only joy," cries Suso, "the way in which I may bear upon my body the marks of Thy Love."...

The greatest of the contemplative saints, far from leaving purgation behind them in their progress, were increasingly aware
of their own inadequateness, the nearer they approached to the
unitive state.... In this sense, then, purification is a perpetual
process. That which mystical writers mean, however, when they
speak of the Way of Purgation, is rather the slow and painful
completion of Conversion. It is the drastic turning of the self
from the unreal to the real life: a setting of her house in order,
an orientation of the mind to Truth.

"The essence of purgation," says Richard of St. Victor, "is self-
simplification." Nothing can happen until this has proceeded a
certain distance: till the involved interests and tangled motives of
the self are simplified, and the false complications of temporal life
are recognized and cast away.   — *Mysticism*

DETACHMENT

By *Poverty* the mystic means an utter self-stripping, the casting
off of immaterial as well as material wealth, a complete detachment from all finite things. By *Chastity* he means an extreme
and limpid purity of soul, cleansed from personal desire and
virgin in all but God; by *Obedience,* that abnegation of selfhood, that mortification of the will, which results in a complete
self-abandonment: a "holy indifference" to the accidents of life.
These three aspects of perfection are really one.... We may therefore treat them as three manifestations of one thing: which thing
is Inward Poverty. "Blessed are the poor in spirit, for theirs is
the Kingdom of Heaven," is the motto of all pilgrims on this
road....

"My little sisters the birds," said St. Francis, greatest adept of
that high wisdom, "Brother Sun, Sister Water, Mother Earth."
Not my servants, but my kindred and fellow-citizens, who may
safely be loved so long as they are not desired....

It is the business of Lady Poverty to confer on her lovers
this freedom of the Universe, to eradicate delusion, cut out the

spreading growth of claimfulness, purify the heart, and initiate them into the "great life of the All...."

The detachment of the mystic is just a restoration to the liberty in which the soul was made: it is a state of joyous humility in which he cries, "Nought I am, nought I have, nought I lack." To have arrived at this is to have escaped from the tyranny of selfhood: to be initiated into the purer air of that universe which knows but one rule of action — that which was laid down once and for all by St. Augustine when he said, in the most memorable and misquoted of epigrams: "Love, and do what you like."

— *Mysticism*

THE ILLUMINATION OF THE SELF

A harmony is thus set up between the mystic and Life in all its forms. Undistracted by appearance, he sees, feels, and knows it in one piercing act of loving comprehension. "And the bodily sight stinted," says Julian [of Norwich], "but the spiritual sight dwelled in mine understanding, and I abode with reverent dread joying in what I saw." The heart outstrips the clumsy senses, and sees — perhaps for an instant, perhaps for long periods of bliss — an undistorted and more veritable world.... The London streets are paths of loveliness; the very omnibuses look like colored archangels, their laps filled full of little trustful souls....

If the Mystic Way be considered as an organic process of transcendence, this illuminated apprehension of things, this cleansing of the doors of perception, is surely what we might expect to occur as man moves toward higher centers of consciousness. ...In such moments of clear sight and enhanced perception as that which Blake and Boehme describe, the mystic and artist do see *sub specie aeternitatis* the Four-Fold River of Life — that World of Becoming in which, as Erigena says, "Every visible and invisible creature is a theophany or appearance of God...."

Sweetly, it is true, the illuminated mystic may live; but not, as some think, placidly. Enlightenment is a symptom of growth and growth is a living process, which knows no rest. The spirit, indeed, is invaded by a heavenly peace; but it is the peace, not of idleness, but of ordered activity. "A rest most busy," in Hilton's words: an appropriation of the Divine. The urgent push of an indwelling spirit, aspiring to its home in the heart of Reality, is felt more and more, as the invasion of the normal consciousness by the transcendental personality — the growth of the New Man — proceeds towards its term.   — *Mysticism*

INTROVERSION: CONTEMPLATION

What, in effect, can they [that is, contemplatives] tell us about the knowledge of reality which they attained in that brief communion with the Absolute?

They tell us chiefly, when we come to collate their evidence, two apparently contradictory things. They speak, almost in the same breath, of an exceeding joy, a Beatific Vision, an intense communion, and a "loving sight": and of an exceeding emptiness, a barren desert, an unfathomable Abyss, a nescience, a Divine Dark. Again and again these pairs of opposites occur in all first-hand descriptions of pure contemplation: Remoteness and Intimacy, Darkness and Light. Bearing in mind that these four metaphors all describe the same process "seen through a temperament," and represent the reaction of that temperament upon Absolute Reality, we may perhaps by their comparison obtain some faint idea of the totality of that indescribable experience at which they hint. . . .

His descriptions will always lean to the impressionistic rather than to the scientific side. The "deep yet dazzling darkness," the "unfathomable abyss," the Cloud of Unknowing, the "embrace of the Beloved," all represent not the Transcendent but his relation with the Transcendent; not an object observed, but an overwhelming impression felt, by the totality of his being during his communion with a Reality which is One.

•

It has become a commonplace with writers on mysticism to say, that all subsequent writers took from Dionysius this idea of "Divine Darkness," and entrance therein as the soul's highest privilege; took it, so to speak, ready-made and on faith, and incorporated it in their tradition. To argue thus is to forget that mystics are above all things practical people. They do not write for the purpose of handing on a philosophical scheme, but in order to describe something which they have themselves experienced; something which they feel to be of transcendent importance for humanity. If, therefore, they persist — and they do persist — in using this simile of "darkness" to describe their experience in contemplation, it can only be because it fits the facts....

What, then, do those who use this image of the "dark" really mean by it? They mean this: that God in His absolute Reality is unknowable — is dark — to man's intellect: which is, as Bergson has reminded us, adapted to other purposes than those of divine intuition. When, under the spur of mystic love, the whole personality of man comes into contact with that reality, it enters a plane of experience to which none of the categories of the intellect apply. Reason finds itself, in a most actual sense, "in the dark" — immersed in the Cloud of Unknowing. This dimness and lostness of the mind, then, is a necessary part of the mystic's ascent to the Absolute.   — *Mysticism*

THE DARK NIGHT OF THE SOUL

All these forms of the Dark Night — the "Absence of God," the sense of sin, the dark ecstasy, the loss of the self's old passion, peace and joy, and its apparent relapse to lower spiritual and

mental levels — are considered by the mystics themselves to con-
stitute aspects or parts of one and the same process: the final
purification of the will or stronghold of the personality, that it
may be merged without any reserve "in God where it was first."
The function of this episode of The Mystic Way is to cure the soul
of the innate tendency to seek and rest in spiritual joys; to con-
fuse Reality with the joy given by the contemplation of Reality. It
is the completion of that ordering of disordered loves, that trans-
valuation of values, with which the Way of Purgation began. A
total abandonment of the individualistic standpoint, of that trivial and egotistic quest of personal satisfaction which thwarts the
great movement of the Flowing Light, is the supreme condition
of man's participation in Reality....

The various torments and desolations of the Dark Night con-
stitute this last and drastic purgation of the spirit; the doing away
of separateness, the annihilation of selfhood, even though all that
self now claims for its own be the Love of God.   — *Mysticism*

THE UNITIVE LIFE

We are then one and all the kindred of the mystics; and it is by
dwelling upon this kinship, by interpreting — so far as we may —
their great declarations in the light of our little experience, that
we shall learn to understand them best. Strange and far away
though they seem to us, they are not cut off from us by some
impassable abyss. They belong to us....

To be a mystic is simply to participate here and now in that
real and eternal life; in the fullest, deepest sense which is possible to man. It is to share, as a free and conscious agent — not
a servant, but a son — in the joyous travail of the Universe: its
mighty onward sweep through pain and glory towards its home
in God.... The mystic act of union, that joyous loss of the transfigured self in God, which is the crown of man's conscious ascent
towards the Absolute, is the contribution of the individual to this,
the destiny of the Cosmos.

The mystic knows that destiny. It is laid bare to his lucid vision, as our puzzling world of form and color is to normal sight.... He is the pioneer of Life on its age-long voyage to the One: and shows us, in his attainment, the meaning and value of that life.   — *Mysticism*

DIVINE FECUNDITY

Like the story of the Cross, so too the story of man's spirit ends in a garden: in a place of birth and fruitfulness, of beautiful and natural things. Divine Fecundity is its secret: existence, not for its own sake, but for the sake of a more abundant life. It ends with the coming forth of divine humanity, never again to leave us: living in us, and with us, a pilgrim, a worker, a guest at our table, a sharer at all hazards in life. The mystics witness to this story: waking very early they have run on before us, urged by the greatness of their love. We, incapable as yet of this sublime encounter, looking in their magic mirror, listening to their stammered tidings, may see far off the consummation of the race.

— *Mysticism*

GLORIFIED

Life is not life if it be not life from death. And God is not God if He be not the end of men.   — Karl Barth

When the evening of life comes, you will be judged on love.
                                        — St. John of the Cross

At the heart of Christianity, the clue to its astonishing history and persistent power, we find a contrast, a crisis, a transformation. The contrast is between the life before and after Calvary. The crisis which marks the transition is the Passion; that great gesture of unblemished charity in which, as St. John says, we know love. The transformation is that of man's limited nature, his narrow self, as we know it here, into something new, strange, and lovely; possessed of a mysterious power and freedom, a fresh kind of life, and spending this life within our everyday existence to serve and save men. Only a spiritual sequence which is completed in this life-giving life is fully sane and fully Christian. The Pattern which is shown to us is a pattern which lives and moves and changes as we must live and move and change.

Those who give themselves to the life of the spirit are brought bit by bit, as they can bear it and respond to it, to that crisis in which all that they have won seems taken away from them; and they are faced by the demand for complete self-surrender, an act of unconditional trust. But this is not the end of the story. The self-abandonment of the Cross is a transition from the half-real to the real; it is the surrender of our separate self-hood, even our spiritual self-hood — the last and the most difficult offering of love — so that we may enter by this strait gate, so hard to find and so unpromising in appearance, that life-giving life of triumphant charity for which humanity is made. Only those who are generous up to the limits of self-loss can hope to become channels of the generosity of God. In that crisis the I, the separate self, with its loves and hates, its personal preoccupations, is sacrificed and left behind. And out of this most true and active death to self, the spirit is reborn into the real life: not in some other transcendental world, but in this world, among those who love us and those we love.

•

So the Crucifix, which is the perfect symbol of generous sacrifice, is the perfect symbol of victory too: of the love which shirks nothing and so achieves everything, the losing and the finding of life. "He was crucified, dead, and buried — rose again and ascended." With this double statement the Creed, the rule of prayer, reaches its climax, and shows us in a sentence the deepest meaning of our life: declaring in plain language that unlimited self-offering is the only path from man to God.

This means that the Thought of God, penetrating our tangled world and entering into union with our imperfect nature, saves and transforms that nature, raises it to a new level, not by power, but by the complete exercise of courageous love; the deliberate facing of the world's worst. And we, following the footsteps of that holy life which reveals reality, must take the same way. "As dying and behold we live" is a literal fact for the genuine Christian. The release of power, the transformation of life which comes from unconditional self-abandonment, is guaranteed to us by the story of Easter and the Forty Days: its continuance in the sacraments and the saints. We too achieve all by risking all. Christianity is a triumphant heroism. The valiant obedience of the Blessed Virgin makes the Incarnation possible: the more complete and awful self-giving of the Cross makes the life-giving life of the Church and the saints possible. The ancient Easter sequence sums it up:

> Death and Life strove together in awful combat;
> The Lord of Life, who died, living reigns.

And yet this reign, by its strange triumphant beauty, is not manifested in any of the sensational incidents of which Apocalyptic writers had dreamed; by a sudden coming in the Clouds of Heaven, or by the shattering of our ordinary human world. Still true to the Divine method of hiddenness and humility, it comes back into that world very quietly; brought by love, and only recognized by love. It appears by preference in connection with the simple realities of everyday existence, and exercises its enlightening, pacifying, strengthening influence in and through these homely realities. Personal needs, friendly affections, become the consecrated channels of the immortal Love, which declares its victories by a quiet and tender benediction poured out on ordinary life. The glory of the Divine Humanity is not shown in the Temple and the Synagogue. He seeks out his nervous followers within the arena of ordinary life; meets them behind the locked doors of the Upper Room, waits for them in the early morning by the lake side, walks with them on the country road, and suddenly discloses Himself in the breaking of the bread. The characters of the old life which are carried through into this new and glorified life are just those which express a homely and cherishing love. It is the One who had fed the multitude, pacified the distracted, washed the dusty feet of His followers, and given Himself to be their food, who now re-enters their troubled lives; for their sake, not for his own.

•

For us, these scenes have an other-worldly beauty. We see them bathed in the supernatural light. But for Peter and Thomas, James and John, they happened under normal conditions of time and place. Frightened, weary and discouraged, worried about the future and remorseful about the past, for them the wonder abode in the quiet return of the Holy and Immortal who was yet the familiar and the human, to the commonplace surroundings in which they had known Him best. Silently disregarding their disappointing qualities, their stupidity, cowardice, and lack of trust, He came back to them in a pure impetus of charity; came down to their level as one that serveth, making visible the Invisible Love, and gave the guarantee which their petty standards demanded and their narrow souls could apprehend. Thus, by this unblemished courtesy, "binding His majesty to our lowliness," as the Byzantine liturgy says, He restored their faith, hope, and charity; and gave them an example only less searching in its self-oblivious gentleness than the lesson of the washing of the feet.

Even their own fragmentary notes of what happened, or seemed to them to happen, shame and delight us by their witness to the splendor and humility of generous love. "My Lord!" says St. Thomas, seeing, touching, and measuring the Holiness so meekly shown to him in his own crude terms; and then, passing beyond that sacramental revelation to the unseen, untouched, unmeasured, uttering the word every awakened soul longs to utter — "My God!" The very heart of the Christian revelation is disclosed in that scene.

•

So it is that the real mark of spiritual triumph — the possession of that more lovely, more abundant life which we discern in moments of deep prayer — is not an abstraction from this world, but a return to it; a willing use of its conditions as material for the expression of love. There is nothing high-minded about Christian holiness. It is most at home in the slum, the street, the hospital ward: and the mysteries through which its gifts are distributed are themselves chosen from amongst the most homely realities of life. A little water, some fragments of bread, and a chalice of wine are enough to close the gap between two worlds; and give soul and senses a trembling contact with the Eternal Charity. By means of these its creatures, that touch still cleanses, and that hand still feeds. The serene, unhurried, self-imparting which began before Gethsemane continues still. Either secretly or sacramentally, every Christian is a link in the chain of perpetual penitents and perpetual communicants through which the rescuing Love reaches out to the world. Perhaps there is no more certain mark of a mature spirituality than the way in which those who possess it are able to enter a troubled situation and say, "Peace," or turn from the exercise of heroic love to meet the humblest needs of men.

•

One of the few passages of spiritual value in the Apocryphal Gospels, and the only one that has left its mark on the Creed, is that which describes the coming of the soul of Christ into the unseen world of the departed: His "descent into hell" to the rescue of those "spirits in prison" to whom the revelation of the Divine Charity had not been given on earth. Some of the greatest of the medieval painters have found in that story the perfect image of triumphant love. They show us the liberated soul of Jesus, robed in that humanity which has endured the anguish of the Passion, passing straight from this anguish into the delighted exercise of a saving charity. He comes with an irresistible rush, bearing the banner of redemption to the imprisoned souls of those who knew him not. There they are, pressing forward to the mouth of the cave; the darkness, narrowness, and unreality from which he comes to free them, at His own great cost. The awed delight of the souls He rescues is nothing beside the Rescuer's own ecstatic delight. It is as if the charity self-given on Calvary could not wait a moment, but rushed straight to the awaiting joy of releasing the souls of men. There is no hint of the agony and darkness through which he has won the power to do this. Everything is forgotten but the need which the Rescuer is able to meet. That scene, if we place it — as we should do — before the lovely story of Easter and the Forty Days, helps us to an understanding of their special quality; and sets before us once for all Rescuing Love as the standard of Christian holiness, and its production in us as the very object of our transformation. For this is our tiny share in that Divine action which brings the supernatural charity right down into the confusions and sorrows of our life, to "save" and transform. Here we look at Sanctity, that "risen life" which has power, and triumphs in virtue of its love. And the deepest truth about ourselves is, that we are human beings; and therefore have in ourselves the capacity for this same triumph of the power that is love, if we are willing to face the cost. The cost is that crucifying struggle with natural self-love, that passive endurance of the Divine action, which brings the soul out of the narrow, intense, individual life — even though it be apparently religious life into the wide self-spending universal life — of the Divine Charity. "We know that we have passed out of death into life, because we love the brethren." But tension, suffering, and utter helplessness mark that crucial change.

When Christ said, "My Father and your Father — My God and your God," He made a declaration which must enslave and transfigure the whole lives of those who realize what is implied in it; conferring on them the tremendous privilege of partnership. "Fellow-workers with God, because co-heirs with Christ." After that, the soul's own life is to be "in the Spirit": that is, delivered from the tension and struggle of those who are ever striving to adjust the claims of two worlds, because gladly subordinated to the mighty purposes of God. Everything is left behind which does not contribute to those purposes; and so, all that is left is harmonized within His peace. To them that are perishing, says St. Paul, such a program is foolishness: "but unto us which are being saved it is the Power of God." It is, in fact, what Christianity really means; and if Christians chose to stand up to this obligation, they could transform the world.

"Where the Spirit of the Father is," said St. Irenaeus, "there is a Living Man: living because of his share in the Spirit, man because of the substance of his flesh." Other men are, at best, half alive. And the Spirit of the Father is Creative Love. That is the fundamental quality which man shares with God, and which constitutes his kinship with God. Where this rules his life he becomes, in one way or another, an agent of the Eternal Charity. That of course in its perfection is the secret of the Saints; the cause of what we call their "supernatural power."

"My Father and your Father" means, then, that we are the children of the Eternal Perfect, Whose essential nature is generous Love; and that we are destined to manifest the splendor of God in and through the homely scenes, the long and arduous labors, self-givings, and sufferings, which the Divine Wisdom irradiated once and irradiates still. It means a new quality of life possible to us and awaiting us; not somewhere else, but where we are now.

•

This quality of life is already manifest, wherever the limiting forms of human devotion, human service are given in simplicity to the total purposes of God. For reality has been shown to us incarnate among men, so that we may try to weave its pattern into the texture of human life; redeeming that life from ugliness and making it a garment of God. It is not a conspicuous pattern. The shimmer of holiness appears upon the surface mostly in obscure acts of sacrifice and quiet selfless deeds. But when we look behind, and trace this delicate beauty to its source, what we see is a living Love; so individual, and yet so general, that on one hand the relation of each spirit to that Spirit is unique and complete, and on the other the love poured out on one subtracts nothing from the love given to all.

To realize this is already to move out from the narrow experience of the pious individualist, absorbed in the contemplation of his own spiritual shortcomings and desires, to the glorious liberty of those whose life is cleansed of all self-occupation, and flows out in delighted response to the demand of God and the needs of man: "being made the children of God and of light," as the baptismal service has it. Our petty worries, faults, anxieties, and ignorances, our careful discriminations in practice and belief, even our deplorable rebellions and antipathies fade and shrivel when we see our total destiny like this, and sink our small efforts in the tide of the Eternal Spirit's life. We taste then, in our limited way, something of that experience which transfigured the Twelve; imparted to them the life-giving life, and sent them out to spread it through the world.

And indeed, the Christian is required for this and for no other purpose; to be one more worker for the Kingdom, one more transmitter of the Divine Charity, the great spendthrift action of God. From the first, the transmitters have been ordinary faulty people like ourselves. "He gave himself in either kind," not to a select company of sanctified souls, but to unstable Peter, dubious Thomas, pushful James and John; Paul, who had persecuted Him as sincerely and as savagely as any modern rationalist, and who had consented to His martyr's death. They must have seemed a very unlikely collection. But they were surrendered, and so they could be used; woven into the tissue of that Church which transmits the triumphant and all-sacrificing life.

•

That life indwells the world and the world knows it not; largely because those to whom it is given fail to disclose it. Christians, that "nation" as the New Testament calls them, who exist only to be the wide-open channels of the inpouring Spirit of Charity, block its passage by their interior hardness, their spiritual selfishness, apathy, love of comfort, their petty and sterile religious outlook. They are too timid, too canny, to risk losing their own lives; to give themselves with undemanding generosity, in order to find the all-generous Life of God.

It is easy enough to appreciate the lovely vision of that all-generous Life, poured out through human channels to transform the life of men. All our religious pussy cats can enjoy the beauty of the design, and bask in the golden light which illuminates it. Their vague idealism and fussy optimism and sentimental other-worldliness all feel warmer and brighter when that radiance falls upon them. But they do not care to face the fact that the design is a working-drawing, which we are required to carry out with the homely materials at hand. The worth of men is not judged by their admiration of its beauty, but by the perfection with which it is reproduced within their own lives. That which we are shown in contemplation we are required to express in action: not by our peculiar beliefs and punctual religious practices, but simply by the exercise of Rescuing Love.

•

The immortal figure of Christ, God's pattern for humanity, stands over against life; and judges it by irradiating it. He sets the standard, shows what man is meant to be; revealing Himself in every demand on our generosity, however homely, and by that demand alone and our response to it separating the real from the unreal, the living from the dead. Yet in the deepest sense, even that response is not truly our own. It is the One God, indwelling in His deep humanity His little human creatures, Who stirs in us and initiates each movement of Charity; "secretly inciting," says von Hügel, "what He openly crowns."

And now we begin to see a certain sequence in those mysteries through which His Reality is brought into focus for us; or, in the language of theology, the Word is made flesh. That sequence begins where life begins right down in the natural order, leaving no phase of our common experience outside the radiance of love. It develops among homely things, quietly, slowly, and without sensational incidents; subject to all the common tests, strains, joys, and duties of our human existence, and through and within them increasing in wisdom and stature. Confronted in the deep solitude of the wilderness by man's crucial choice between self-interest and self-loss, this Life rejects everything that is less than God; everything that ministers to self-will. So, emerging into the unsullied light of truth it manifests truth; teaching the Will of God for men, and the path men must follow to God. And because this is the life of One who sees men as they are, knowing what is in man, there pours out through it that wide, loving, and creative compassion which is the only source of healing and of help. By the interplay of that pure truth and that warm compassion, it becomes filled with a rescuing and redeeming Power, which transcends difficulties and does not notice dangers; and this Power is made perfect in sacrifice — the Eucharist, Gethsemane, and the Cross. Thus by a path which never departs from the human landscape we are led out and up beyond the human landscape, to a Divine revelation that yet is deeply human, and a human revelation that is completely Divine.

— The School of Charity

5

Worship

Worship (1937) is Underhill's last major study. In the following three selections, the mature Underhill can be heard. She speaks with the voice of a devout liturgical churchwoman who treasures the paschal mystery. Notice that corporate worship is one of her principal concerns. While much of her earlier writing, about the mystical life, had a distinctly personal and private character, her tone in Worship *is very much that of the Christian in community.*

THE NATURE OF WORSHIP

Worship, in all its grades and kinds, is the response of the creature to the Eternal: nor need we limit this definition to the human sphere. There is a sense in which we may think of the whole life of the Universe, seen and unseen, conscious and unconscious, as an act of worship, glorifying its Origin, Sustainer, and End. Only in some such context, indeed, can we begin to understand the emergence and growth of the spirit of worship in men, or the influence which it exerts upon their concrete activities. Thus worship may be overt or direct, unconscious or conscious. Where conscious, its emotional color can range from fear through reverence to self-oblivious love. But whatever its form of expression may be, it is always a subject-object relationship; and its general existence therefore constitutes a damaging criticism of all merely subjective and immanent explanations of Reality. For worship is an acknowledgment of Transcendence; that is to say, of a Reality independent of the worshiper, which is always more or less deeply colored by mystery, and which is there first. As von Hügel would say, it is "rooted in ontology": or, if we prefer the witness of a modern anthropologist, even on primitive levels it at least points to man's profound sense of dependence upon "the spiritual side of the unknown" (R. R. Marett, *Sacraments of Simple Folk*). So, directly we take this strange thing Worship seriously, and give it the status it deserves among the various responses of men to their environment, we find that it obliges us to take up a particular attitude toward that environment. Even in its crudest form, the law of prayer — indeed the fact of prayer — is already the law of belief; since humanity's universal instinct to worship cannot be accounted for, if naturalism tells the whole truth about life. That instinct means the latent recognition of a metaphysical reality, standing over against physical reality, which men are driven to adore, and long to apprehend. In other words it is the implicit, even though unrecognized Vision of God — that disclosure of the Supernatural which is overwhelming, self-giving, and attractive all at once — which is the first cause of all worship, from the puzzled upward glance of the primitive to the delighted self-oblation of the saint. Here, the human derived spirit perceives and moves towards its Origin and goal; even though that perception shares the imperfections and uncertainties of the temporal order, and is often embodied in crude and mistaken forms. Here man responds to the impact of Eternity, and in so doing learns the existence of Eternity; accepting his tiny place in that secret life of Creation, which consists in the praise, adoration, and manifestation of God. That is to say, he achieves his destiny.

These words, of course, are written from the standpoint of Christian Theism. Such a view of worship implies a developed religion; but it is a function of developed religion to speak for and interpret the inarticulate convictions of the race. It is possible to regard worship as one of the greatest of humanity's mistakes;

a form taken by the fantasy-life, the desperate effort of bewildered creatures to come to terms with the surrounding mystery. Or it may be accepted as the most profound of man's responses to reality; and more than this, the organ of his divine knowledge and the earnest of eternal life. Between these two extreme positions, however, it is difficult to find a firm resting place for the mind. Nor has the religious man any choice. He is bound to take worship seriously, and ever more seriously with the deepening of his own spiritual sense. It points steadily toward the Reality of God: gives, expresses, and maintains that which is the essence of all sane religion — a theocentric basis to life. "The first or central act of religion is *adoration,* sense of God, His otherness though nearness, His distinctness from all finite beings, though not separateness — aloofness — from them" (von Hügel, *Selected Letters*).

•

It is true that from first to last self-regarding elements are mixed with human worship; but these are no real part of it. Not man's needs and wishes, but God's presence and incitement, first evoke it. As it rises towards purity and leaves egotistic piety behind, He becomes more and more the only Fact of existence, the one Reality; and the very meaning of Creation is seen to be an act of worship, a devoted proclamation of the splendor, the wonder, and the beauty of God. In this great *Sanctus,* all things justify their being and have their place. God alone matters, God alone Is — creation only matters because of Him. "Wherein does your prayer consist?" said St. John of the Cross to one of his penitents. She replied: "In considering the Beauty of God, and in rejoicing that He has such beauty."

Such disinterested delight is the perfection of worship. Yet we cannot limit the word to that small group of souls capable of this effect of Charity, or even to those activities which it is usual to class as "religious." Though we find at its heart the adoring response of spirit to Spirit, its periphery is great enough to include all the expressive acts and humble submissions of men, if they

are given a Godward orientation. The great outbursts of unshak-
able certitude and adoring love which we find upon the lips of
the Saints stand up like Alpine peaks in the spiritual landscape of
humanity. But the lower pastures, the deepest valleys and dark-
est forests, even the jungles and the swamps, are all part of the
same world; depend on the same given heat and light, the same
seasonal vicissitudes. Each in its own way responds to that heat
and light, and under its incitement brings forth living things.

We shall not understand the mountain by treating it in isolation; nor do justice to the lower levels unless we also remember
the heights. "God," says St. John of the Cross again, "passes
through the thicket of the world, and wherever His glance falls
He turns all things to beauty."

Worship, then, at every level, always means God and the
priority of God; however thick the veils through which He is ap-
prehended, and however grotesque the disguise He may seem to
wear. Through and in a multitude of strange divinities and along
lowly channels suited to the lowliness of man, the "outpouring
of the Incomprehensible Grandeur," as Dionysius the Areopagite
says, goes on.

We in our worshiping action are compelled to move within
the devotional sphere, with all its symbolic furniture, its archaic
survivals, its pitfalls, its risks of sentimentalism, herd-suggestion,
and disguised self-regard. But the mighty Object of our worship
stands beyond and over against all this in His utter freedom and
distinctness. "Can" and "cannot," "is" and "is not" must not
be predicated of Him, without a virtual remembrance that these
words merely refer to our limited experience and not to God
as He is in Himself. If this contrast is forgotten, we shall never
understand the religious scene and the strange objects with which
it is bestrewn.

There is no department of life which asks from those who
study it so much humble sympathy, such a wide, genial, un-
fastidious spirit, or so constant a remembrance of our own
limitations as this; nor one in which it is more necessary to remember the wholesome reminder of the psychologist that we

ourselves, however apparently civilized, are still possessed of a primitive subconsciousness which is nowhere more active than in the practices of our religion.

•

If the first point about worship is its theocentric character, if its reference be always to "the Absolute and Eternal, standing beyond the present and the past" (Nicolas of Cusa, *The Vision of God*), there follows from this the obvious truth that man could never have produced it in his own strength. It does not appear spontaneously from within the created order, and cannot be accounted for in terms of evolution. Strictly speaking, there is no such thing as "natural religion": the distinction which is often drawn between "natural" and "revealed" faith is an artificial one, set up by theologizing minds. That awed conviction of the reality of the Eternal over against us, that awareness of the Absolute, that sense of God, which in one form or another is the beginning of all worship, whether it seems to break in from without, or to arise within the soul, does not and cannot originate in man. It comes to him where he is, as a message from another order; God disclosing Himself to and in His creation "by diverse portions and in diverse manners" conditioned by the limitations of the humble creature He has made. It is, in fact, a Revelation, proportioned to the capacity of the creature, of something wholly other than our finite selves, and not deducible from our finite experience: the splendor and distinctness of God. Therefore the easy talk of the pious naturalist about man's approach to God, is both irrational — indeed plainly impudent — and irreverent; unless the priority of God's approach to man be kept in mind.

In this respect worship stands alone, and cannot be equated with man's other discoveries of, and reactions to, his rich and many-leveled environment. In all these, he is pressed by the needs and perils of his situation, or by the prick of his own desires, first to exploration and then to precarious adjustments with this or that aspect of a changing world. But in his worship, he is

compelled as it were in spite of himself to acknowledge and respond to a Wholeness, a Perfection already fully present over
against him — something, as St. Augustine says, "insusceptible
of change." This contrast between the successive and the Eternal lies at the root of all worship, which ever looks away from
the transitory and created to the Abiding and Increate; not because this august Reality consoles or succors men, not because
worship enriches and completes our natural life, but for Its own
sake. Here even the deep religious mood of dependence and of
gratitude must give priority to the fundamental religious mood
of adoration. Where it is emptied of this unearthly element, this
awestruck and creaturely sense of the Holy and Immortal, worship loses its most distinctive characteristic. The Seraphic hymn
gives its very essence: "Holy! holy! holy! Lord God of hosts,
heaven and earth are full of thy glory. Glory be to thee, O Lord
Most High." That is worship.

•

It is true that this holy Reality is at first recognized by man
in a very imperfect and distorted way; and acknowledged in
acts which may bear little apparent resemblance to the practices which we regard as religious. Yet already these acts have
the distinctive mark of worship. They point beyond the world
and natural life, to an independent Object of adoration. That
Transcendent Object, even though conceived as the Cause of all
natural good, and present in and with the natural scene, yet
speaks to man from a realm that exceeds and stands over against
all natural good; and may incite him to deeds and renunciations
which sharply oppose the interests of his natural life, and have
no meaning save in so far as they point beyond the world. As
man develops, its attraction and its pressure are more and more
realized in contrast to those natural interests. And at last in the
Saint (without whose existence worship can never be understood)
the revealed Reality fills the horizon and becomes the sole object
of love; so that even though God gave nothing of Himself to the
soul, yet the soul must give the whole of itself to Him.

It follows from this that worship and prayer, though their relation be so close, and their overlapping so frequent, must never be treated as equivalents. For worship is essentially disinterested — it "means only God" — but prayer is only in some of its aspects disinterested. One offers, the other asks. "What shall I say, my God, my Holy Joy!" exclaims St. Augustine. There is the voice of worship. "Without thy visitation I cannot live!" says Thomas à Kempis. There is the voice of prayer. It is true that throughout the history of religion there has always been a mingling of motives; fear and anxiety, over against the all-powerful Unknown, expressed in propitiation and demand, are inevitable elements of the primitive response; and have endured to affect the whole religious history of the race. But as the genuine religious impulse becomes dominant, adoration more and more takes charge. "I come to seek God because I need Him," may be an adequate formula for prayer. "I come to adore His splendor, and fling myself and all that I have at His feet," is the only possible formula for worship. Even on the crudest levels, it has in it the seed of contemplation, and points towards self-loss.

•

Thus worship will include all those dispositions and deeds which adoration wakes up in us, all the responses of the soul to the Uncreated, all the Godward activities of man. Because it sets the awful Perfection of God over against the creature's imperfection, it becomes the most effective cause of "conviction of sin," and hence of the soul's penitence and purification; here disclosing its creative and transfiguring power. So, too, that strange impulse to sacrifice and unlimited self-abandonment, which is the life-blood of religion, is an expression of the worshiping instinct, and has no meaning except in relation to a supernatural goal. When we consider how unnecessary religious action is to man's physical well-being — how frequently, indeed, its demands run counter to his material advantage — yet how irresistible is its attraction for awakened souls, we can hardly doubt that here in this mysterious intercourse which we know from the human side as "worship,"

there is disclosed to us a deep purpose of the Eternal Will, and a
path is opened along which our conditioned spirits can move out
towards the Absolute Life.

Yet having said this, so rich and complex are those spiritual
currents which penetrate and surround us, and so firm the refusal
of Spirit to fit into the neat categories of thought, that we are
bound to qualify the stress upon Transcendence by an acknowledgment of the many strands which enter into the worshiping life;
the many paths along which God makes His approach to man,
and stirs man to respond to His attraction. We are not Deists.
Our worship is of a God Who acts, a Living One Who transcends
what seem to us to be His laws, and has a definite relation with
His creatures; One, too, who works in the depths of our being,
and is self-revealed through His action in history and in nature,
as well as in the soul....

•

The acknowledgment of our total dependence on this free action
of God immanent and transcendent, is therefore a true part of
worship. It follows that, wherever the envisaged end is not man's
comfort, security, or personal success, but His glory and purpose,
the more perfect doing of His Will, then the prayer of petition
itself — e.g., for the graces of the spiritual life, the rescue and
sanctifying of individuals, or the victory of good causes — becomes a true "hallowing of the Name."* In fact the trustful and
childlike demand is itself an act of homage, in so far as it has
the color of adoration: "The eyes of all wait on thee, O Lord;
and thou givest them their meat in due season." As the spiritual
life develops, so this sense of the priority of the Divine action,
the total dependence of the derived spirit on the Absolute Spirit,
deepens; and God, working with and in His creature, though

---

*Thus the Eucharistic prayer of preparation, "Cleanse the thoughts of our hearts
by the inspiration of thy Holy spirit, that we may perfectly love thee and worthily
magnify thy holy name," is both supplication and worship, since its declared object
is the greater glory of God.

often secretly and in disguise, is recognized as the only author of all the supernatural actions of the soul.

This, if at one end worship is lost in God and is seen to be the substance of Eternal Life, so that all our attempts to penetrate its mystery must end in acknowledgment of defeat; at the other end, it broadens out to cover and inform the whole of man's responses to Reality — his total Godward life, with its myriad graded forms of expression, some so crude and some so lovely, some so concrete and some so otherworldly, but all so pathetic in their childishness. Here we obtain a clue to the real significance of those rituals and ceremonies common to almost every creed, which express the deep human conviction that none of the serial events and experiences of human life are rightly met, unless brought into relation with the Transcendent: that all have more than a natural meaning, and must be sanctified by reference to the unseen Powers. Hence the solemn rites which hallow the achievement of adolescence, the blessings of ruler, traveler, bride and bridegroom, the churching of women, ceremonial care for the dead. All these, together with the benediction of house, fields, food, instruments of labor, or badges of service, are to be regarded as acts of worship: for they refer to God as a distinct yet present Reality, and acknowledge His hallowing action and unlimited claim. So, too, the adoring recognition of God in and through nature — in so far as this is not the mere sentimental enjoyment of a pious pantheism — may be a real part, though never the whole, of a worshiping life; for in such a case the visible world, or some aspect of that world, becomes a sacramental revelation of an invisible Reality. Also that total and selfless devotion to the interests of truth or of beauty, which is the impelling cause of the scholar's or the artist's career, has a religious character, and is in essence a response to revelation: for worship has not reached its term until it knows God as no less truly the ultimate Source, Sustainer, and End of perfect Beauty and of utter Truth than of complete Goodness and of purest Self-Donation. Yet all these would lose significance and fall to the natural level, were they not lit up and interpreted by the richer and more costly expressions of man's instinct for God: the long strange history of sacrifice, the dedicated life, and all those "useless" austerities and renunciations which so greatly vex the practical mind. For in these we see in its intense form the human soul's acknowledgment of an obligation to the hidden Perfect; the generous and disinterested — even though uncomprehended — response of the creature to the secret claim and incitement of God. The crude form which this response has often taken should not blind us to its cardinal importance for an understanding of the spiritual situation of man.

And next, if human worship be essentially theocentric, creaturely, disinterested, the humble and graded response of man the finite to the generous and graded self-revelation of the Infinite God, it requires beyond all this a further character; already inherent in its creatureliness. That is, it must have embodiment, concrete expression....

•

This is why, in every human society which has reached even a rudimentary religious consciousness, worship is given its concrete expression in institutions and in ritual acts: and these institutions and acts become in their turn powerful instruments, whereby the worshiping temper is taught, stimulated, and maintained. The painted cave of those prehistoric worshipers of an unknown God who were "simple-minded enough to give of their best to the supra-sensible powers" (J. B. Pratt, *The Religious Consciousness*), the Pagan temple, the Christian cathedral, are all expressions of the same fundamental human need to incorporate, make visible, the spirit of worship; to lavish skill, labor, and wealth on this most apparently "useless" of all the activities of man. So, too, the ritual chant, with its accompaniment of ceremonial movement and manual acts, is found to exert a stabilizing influence at every level of his religious life. And when this costly and explicit embodiment is lacking, or is rejected where once possessed, and the Godward life of the community is not given some sensible and institutional expression within the social complex, worship seldom develops its full richness and power. It remains thin, abstract, and notional: a tendency, an attitude, a general aspiration, moving alongside human life, rather than in it.

It is true that worship, when thus embodied, loses — or seems to lose — something of its purity; but only then can it take up and use man's various powers and capacities, turning the whole creature toward the Eternal, and thus entering the texture of his natural as well as his supernatural life. Certainly, it is here that we encounter the greatest of the dangers that accompany its long history; the danger that form will smother spirit, ritual action take the place of spontaneous prayer, the outward and visible sign obscure the inward grace. But the risk is one which man is bound to take. He is not "pure" spirit, and is not capable of "pure" spiritual acts. Even though in his worship he moves out toward absolutes, and in and through that worship absolutes are revealed to his soul, it is at his own peril that he leaves the world of sense behind, in his approach to the God Who created and informs it. This humbling truth must govern all his responses to Reality.

And more than this, the prevenient God, Who is the cause and object of his worship, comes to man and awakens him where he is, and is discovered by him first in the mysterious movements of nature. Here, in this infant-school of the emerging human spirit, the Unconditioned meets him under his own conditions; and is disclosed to him in the degree in which he can bear it, embodied in a measure in the finite realities of the surrounding world of sense. He must therefore be found, served, and acknowledged in and through that finite world of sense, which is the appointed sphere of our activity: in time, by means of history and historic institutions, and in space by means of sacred objects and ceremonial acts. Only in so far as man's worship is thus firmly rooted in the concrete here-and-now of our common experience, and accepts the conditions imposed by that experience, will it retain its creaturely quality and develop its full richness and life-changing power. It is, too, from within such embodied adoration,

not in defiance of it, that individual worship emerges and develops best: for great realities, as von Hügel has pointed out,
"though invisible, require for their vivid apprehension an imaginative pictorial embodiment" (von Hügel, *The Mystical Element
of Religion*); and only when thus vividly and realistically appre-
hended, will they fully evoke our worship, and enter the texture
of our life.

The demand and action of religion are and must be on man as
he is: a social, sensuous, and emotional creature keenly aware of
his visible environment, but only half aware of the unseen. Therefore that revelation, that awakening disclosure of the spaceless
God which is the cause of worship, must come to us in space,
the reality and attraction of His eternity must be experienced in
time, if they are indeed to enter and transform our experience.
His workings within history and His approach to men through
man, must be recognized as a true part of His action, and a
true disclosure of His Being; and hence as occasions of our grateful adoration, no less compelling than those glimpses of eternity,
which are sometimes vouchsafed to us. This is why the power and
passion of religion, the incitement to worship, are largely realized
in and through "tradition and institution, in which we invariably
find a most strong insistence on the here-and-now, upon a particular place and a particular time" (von Hügel, *The Reality of
God*): and why the Christian revelation — "God manifest in the
flesh" — is unique in its power of evoking worship and love. Here
the historical embodies the metaphysical, and presents the deep
mysteries of Eternal Life to us in a way that we can apprehend.
This humble acceptance of our situation must also govern our
participation in those symbolic acts and traditional rites which
man has brought forth within his natural environment, to bridge
the gap between sense and soul, and support and express the
spirit of worship.

All this will need further exploration as we go on. But already
at this point the Christian can discern how deep-rooted in the
necessities of our situation, and how far-reaching in their implications, are the great truths which rule his own religious life.

Looking with reverence at this universal fact of worship, he will recognize, even in its humblest beginnings and strangest embodiments, some of the implicits of his faith. For first it means and seeks God alone. . . .

•

So those deep realities which the Christian knows as God, Christ, Spirit, Grace, Church, and Sacrament are already found in many ways and under many disguises, wherever man the worshiper lifts his eyes towards the "spiritual side of the unknown."

And last, though in worship the movement — often slow and halting — is yet on the human side simply and wholly Godwards, and this transcendental, self-oblivious undemanding temper must never be discredited or ignored, there remains the question of the effect upon man himself of this deep action of the soul. Why are we called and pressed to it? Is it, ultimately, for our sake? How does it enter into the creative plan?

First, perhaps, we are called to worship because this is the only safe, humble, and creaturely way in which men can be led to acknowledge and receive the influence of an objective Reality. The tendency of all worship to decline from adoration to demand, and from the supernatural to the ethical, shows how strong a pull is needed to neutralize the anthropocentric trend of the human mind; its intense preoccupation with the world of succession, and its own here-and-now desires and needs. And only in so far as it is released from this petty subjectivism, can it hope to grow up into any knowledge of the massive realities of that spiritual universe in which we live and move. It is the mood of deep admiration, the meek acknowledgment of mystery, the humble and adoring gaze, which makes us capable of this revelation.

Worship, then, is an avenue which leads the creature out from his inveterate self-occupation to a knowledge of God, and ultimately to that union with God which is the beatitude of the soul; though we are never to enter on it for this, or any other reason which is tainted by self-regard. We see in its first beginnings man's emerging recognition of the Living Will which is the cause of all his living; and the gradual deepening and widening of this recognition, in diverse ways and manners, till at last all ways and manners are swallowed up in a self-giving love. By this door and this alone, humanity enters into that great life of the spiritual universe which consists in the ceaseless proclamation of the Glory of God.

•

Thus worship purifies, enlightens, and at last transforms, every life submitted to its influence: and this not merely in the ethical or devotional sense. It does all this, because it wakes up and liberates that "seed" of supernatural life, in virtue of which we are spiritual beings, capable of responding to that God Who is Spirit; and which indeed gives to humanity a certain mysterious kinship with Him. Worship is therefore in the deepest sense creative and redemptive. Keeping us in constant remembrance of the Unchanging and the Holy, it cleanses us of subjectivism, releases us from "use and wont" and makes us realists. God's invitation to it and man's response, however limited, crude, or mistaken this response may be, are the appointed means whereby we move towards our true destiny.

Only in so far as this adoring acknowledgment of Reality more and more penetrates his life, does man himself become real; finding within himself the answer to the great Eucharistic prayer, "Make us living men!" and entering by way of unconditioned self-oblation upon the inheritance of Eternal Life. Each separate soul thus transfigured by the spirit of selfless adoration advances that transfiguration of the whole universe which is the Coming of the Kingdom of God. Further discussion of this august theme lies outside the scope of the present work; yet it is well to remind ourselves that worship, though the whole man of sense and spirit, feeling, thought, and will, is and must be truly concerned in it, is above all the work of that mysterious "ground" of our being, that sacred hearth of personality, where the created spirit of man adheres to the increate Spirit of God.   — Worship

THE PRINCIPLES
OF CORPORATE WORSHIP

The worshiping life of the Christian, while profoundly personal, is essentially that of a person who is also a member of a group. In this, of course, it reproduces on spiritual levels the twofold character of his natural life; disciplined and supported by the social framework, to which each of its members has a personal responsibility and makes a personal contribution, but inwardly free. The Christian as such cannot fulfil his spiritual obligations in solitude. He forms part of a social and spiritual complex with a new relation to God; an organism which is quickened and united by that Spirit of supernatural charity which sanctifies the human race from above, and is required to incarnate something of this supernatural charity in the visible world. Therefore even his most lonely contemplations are not merely a private matter; but always to be regarded in their relation to the purpose and action of God Who incites them, and to the total life of the Church....

The corporate life of worship has therefore an importance far exceeding the personal salvation or blessedness of the individual worshipers, or the devotional opportunity which it gives to them. It stands for the total orientation of life towards God; expressed both through stylized liturgical action, and spontaneous common praise. Moreover the personal relation to God of the individual — his inner life — is guaranteed and kept in health by his social relation to the organism, the spiritual society, the Church....

•

The Christian liturgy — taking this word now in its most general sense — is the artistic embodiment of this social yet personal life. Here we are not concerned with its historic origins, its doctrinal implications, or the chief forms it has assumed in the course of its development: but simply with its here-and-now existence, value, and meaning as the ordered framework of the Church's corporate worship, the classic medium by which the ceaseless adoring action of the Bride of Christ is given visible and audible expression. It is plain that the living experience of this whole Church, visible and invisible, past and present, stretched out in history and yet poised on God, must set the scene for Christian worship; not the poor little scrap of which any one soul, or any sectional group, is capable. Thus there must be a traditional worshiping act of the Church, a great liturgical life, of which the sectional worship of its various groups and branches will form a part, and to which the many-leveled action of its isolated members with all their varying moods and insights contributes an act which includes and harmonizes all apparent differences, looking ever more and more toward that perfected heavenly life of adoration where these differences vanish in the single movement of all loving souls towards "the Abiding, the Prevenient, the Beginning and the End and Crown of light and life and love" (von Hügel, *The Reality of God*). This total liturgical life of the *Corpus Christi* is not merely a collection of services, offices, and sacraments. Deeply considered, it is the sacrificial life of Christ Himself; the Word indwelling His Church, gathering in His eternal priestly action the small Godward movements, sacrifices, and aspirations of "all the broken and the meek" (von Hügel, *Letters to a Niece*), and acting through those ordered signs and sacraments by means of these His members on earth. Whether this Church be given hard and fast juridical boundaries, as in Roman Catholicism, or is seen as a group of autonomous families, as by Anglicans and Orthodox, or, felt to be independent of visible expression, as by Quakers and other Independents, the principle is the same: the eternal self-offering of Christ to God in and through this mystical body.

Hence the corporate worship of the Church is not simply that of an assembly of individuals who believe the same things, and therefore unite in doing the same things. It is real in its own right; an action transcending and embracing all the separate souls taking part in it. The individual as such dies to his separate self-hood — even his spiritual self-hood — on entering the Divine Society: is "buried in baptism" and reborn as a living cell of the Mystical Body of Christ. St. Paul insists again and again on this transfer of status as the essential point about Christianity (cf. Ephesians 1:22, 23; 2:19–22; Colossians 2:10, 13; 3:1–3; etc.).

Therefore the response to God of this whole Body, this supernatural organism, in life and in worshiping acts, is of cardinal importance; and since this response is to take place on earth as in heaven, it must have its here-and-now embodiment — inadequate as this must always be to the supernatural situation it shows forth. Nor should we expect simplicity, clarity, uniformity, to be the marks of this action as seen from our point of view; but rather great diversity of level and function within that one great organism of which no man knows the limits but God alone (1 Corinthians 12).

•

We come down from these thoughts, to consider the outward forms taken by this liturgic life of the Christian Society. Here the Eucharist and the Daily Office stand out from the beginning as the classic expressions of the Church's ordered worship. But we do not get a real view of the situation, unless we add to them another and very different form of expression; the free, enthusiastic, unstylized group worship, the spontaneous response to the stirrings of the Spirit, which began in the childhood of the Church and — now for the most part separated from her liturgical action — has continued in various expressions ever since, sometimes going underground for long periods but sooner or later breaking out with disconcerting vigor and freedom....

Primitive Christian worship was therefore both sacramental and prophetic: and during the early centuries the Church seems to have fluctuated between these ideals. The free and charismatic type with its accompanying difficulties and inconveniences — already manifest in the New Testament (1 Corinthians 12 and 14) — gradually sank into the background of the Christian corporate life. Nevertheless it has never died out, and reappears in every "revival" as a protest against the supposed formality and unreality of the liturgic routine; reasserting the freedom and direct action of the Spirit, the priesthood of the individual, the prophetic office of "preachers of the Word," the call to personal consecration. Wherever the institutional life stiffens and becomes standardized, there is a reaction toward that primitive group enthusiasm and prophetic ministry which is described in the New Testament and — even though it sometimes oversteps the bounds of good taste and common sense — is a true part of the Church's Godward life....

•

It is a tragedy of the Christian life that almost from the first the prophetic and sacramental tempers have tended to separate. For the Catholic and the Orthodox, as for his Roman and Greek and Jewish forbears, the sacrificial act, the oblation with its completion in communion, as the expressive vehicle of man's response to God, is the very essence of public worship. Here we see cultus, with its antique surroundings of sanctuary, altar, and priest, conservers and transmitters of the ritual tradition; changing their form, it is true, under the pressure of history, but again and again reasserting their value and power. Here personal initiative tends to be subordinated to the greater action of the Church, regarded as the organ of grace and redemption. But for the many reforming groups and sects which sprang up inside and outside the borders of the Patristic and medieval Church, and for the Protestant reformers and their descendants, personal experience and personal initiative are of paramount importance. Here the essence of worship is prophetic teaching and spontaneous prayer: the announcement of the Word, and the direct and realistic response of the individual to God. Hence there is a distrust and dislike of the fixed forms and symbolic acts which are required by cultus; an almost nervous fear of all pattern and mechanism as necessarily involving insincerity. Neither ideal is sufficient in itself to satisfy the full possibilities of man's corporate Godward life: and neither can long maintain itself alone.

That Godward life in its wholeness needs and has room for both spontaneity and order, personality and tradition, enthusiasm and mystery, prophecy and sacrifice. The "psalms and spiritual songs" recommended by St. Paul — perhaps as an alternative to wilder forms of expression — the "revelations of the Spirit," the ordered prayer and reading which form an ancient part of the Christian devotional life, and the solemn liturgical "breaking of bread" must all contribute to that total life of adoration in which humanity realizes the freely given Presence of the Holy and makes its small response.

It is therefore of great importance that representatives of these contrasting forms of worship should learn to regard each other with sympathy and respect, and even to practice that difficult degree of generosity, which is willing to be taught by those of whom we do not quite approve. This will only be possible when there is a clear understanding of the part which each plays or should play in the total Christian response to God; and of the fact that this response cannot achieve its full and balanced reality and beauty, unless both order and spontaneity, liturgy and liberty, the ministry of the Word and the ministry of the Sacraments, the work of the prophet and the work of the priest, give it of their best. . . .

•

The earliest picture we possess of Christian cultus is the ideal vision of the Apocalypse (cf. Revelation 4:2–11, 5:8–14, and 7:9–17); and this, when we remember the period from which it comes to us, is astonishing in its liturgical richness. There we already see a developed worship of the whole company of the faithful focused upon the altar. The Object of worship is both transcendent and redemptive; the Eternal and Omnipotent God "which was and which is and which is to come" and His Word, the Lamb that was slain on the altar of humanity, the self-given sacrament of Divine Love. The *Sanctus,* which the Church is to carry through the centuries as the essential formula of her Eucharistic prayer, is already heard as the song of the whole created order: for this worship, beheld in its intensive form in the heavenly world, expands to include the cosmos giving "glory and honor and thanks" to that Will by which all things were, and were created. Everyone is doing something; but all in disciplined subservience to the universal tide of adoration which sets toward "God and the Lamb." The sensible accompaniments of an ordered cultus — music, song, incense, ritual movements, and prostrations — are all there and already taken for granted. The Eucharistic and redemptive references of this sublime picture, its Christocentric characters, are clear; but no less clear is the influence of Jewish sacrificial ideas. Stretching back to the very beginnings of man's worship, and forward to all that worship implies, it links two religious worlds.

When we consider the date of this document (probably about A.D. 95, and possibly a little earlier) and its inclusion in the New Testament Canon, we can hardly deny that liturgical worship — carrying over and using with no sense of impropriety the rich symbolism of the Temple, and involving the disciplined action of all participating in it — is a true part of primitive Christianity; at least in ideal, though we may suppose that the circumstances of the early Church seldom allowed that ideal to find adequate expression. Worship is conceived as a sacrifice eternally present at the heart of reality: a Eucharist in which the unceasing *Tersancta* of the "living creatures" before the throne of God is answered by "every creature which is in heaven and on the earth and such as are in the sea." We understand better the spirit of the early Eucharist, if we keep this scene in mind; and note its contrast with the touching simplicity of the earliest liturgies, which yet preserve a certain homely likeness to the heavenly vision by their association of the *Sanctus* and the Passion in the Eucharistic prayer. The Orthodox Church has kept in a remarkable degree this conception of the ceaseless and ecstatic worship poured out in heavenly places, as the eternal pattern for Christian worship on earth. The songs of the Cherubim and Seraphim are heard throughout her liturgy; and in her adoration she unites herself again and again with the heavenly hosts, reminding us of all that is involved in a complete response to the great command *"Sursum corda!"*

•

With this majestic scene to set the standard, we can now look at the chief forms which the common worship of the Church has assumed in the course of her history; the liturgical type centered on the Eucharist, and the free, prophetic, or non-liturgical type, representing the spontaneous religious movements of the group.

And first we have to consider the practical conditions under which men and women can transcend the apparent isolation of the soul and unite in a common act of worship. Here there seem to be three choices. First, there is the corporate silence which covers and unites all the individual acts of devotion, all the levels of fervor and enlightenment. Quaker worship is the best-known representative of this in its pure form. Secondly, there are the worshiping acts which can be performed either by the leader alone, or the leader and trained assistants, in the name of all present, and to which these join their own worship by intention. ...Thirdly there is the ordered ritual, or liturgy; demanding religious action from sense as well as spirit, and so constructed that all present can take some part in that which is done.... All three methods, either alone or in combination with each other, have always existed and been practiced within Christianity. All are alive today, and all have their usefulness and importance, meeting the needs of various occasions and types of soul:

(A) The place of corporate silence is well marked in the early liturgies; and appears to be intimately connected with the development of the collect, or prayer in which the priest or leader gathered up the inarticulate supplications of the faithful and presented them to God....

It is obvious that such an ordered use of corporate silence, with all its advantages of freedom, sincerity, and inwardness, must enrich and deepen the worshiping life of the Church; and should never have been allowed to fall into desuetude. Here the secret response of each soul to the one Spirit forms as it were a separate thread in the woven garment of the Bride. . . .

(B) The second great type of corporate worship escapes some . . . disadvantages. Here action and speech are delegated to a person or group; the congregation uniting itself by intention to that which is done. Thus a focus is provided, and a certain unity of direction is ensured; and the liturgical action covers and unites the devotion of simple and learned. This very ancient method of prayer is still widely used in various ways in all branches of the Church. It gives to all taking part a certain ordered liberty, and also a certain liturgical support; and allows the use of language, music, and ceremonial which are beyond the capacity of the average worshiper, though not beyond his appreciation. When the Pilgrim Etheria visited Jerusalem, she found that the psalms were sung by a trained choir; as indeed they had been in the Temple worship. Cassian tells us that in the monasteries of the Desert Fathers in the fourth century the Psalter, which formed the substance of the common prayer, was read by one voice to which all listened in deep silence and with absorbed attention; pauses being made for meditation. . . . So, too, the fixed prayers of the Anglican Day Office — and, still more, the extempore prayers of Free Church worship — are with few exceptions recited by the priest or ministers in the name of all.

(C) In spite of certain real advantages as to inwardness, freedom, and sincerity, which are possessed by forms of common worship that either suppress or delegate all ritual acts and leave the congregation to unhindered private prayer, it is evident that the third type of corporate service — the concerted action in which all take a real part — is a more complete act of adoration, more congenial to the Christian spirit, and also more efficacious for the common life, than the silent Meeting, the splendid ceremony in which all is done by a few professionals, the "hearing" of a semi-audible Low Mass, or docile attention to the Minister's extempore prayer. The brave attempt of the Quakers to combine the best characteristics of public and private devotion by means of their ritual silence, and the high religious value and great attraction of Low Mass for souls of a contemplative type, are only the exceptions which prove this law; and even these carry their own dangers and, save in the most carefully instructed, inevitably tend to a subjective and atomistic piety. Though we may allow that all fill a useful place in the Christian organism, and meet the special needs of various types of soul, all fall short of the ideal in which the group as a worshiping unit lifts up its heart to God, each individual contributing his share....

•

This is that "general dance" to which, in the old Cornish carol, Christ calls the soul of man. Thus worship in all its degrees is an education in charity, a purgation of egoism. As it draws nearer God, the Divine Light will itself effect that purification. But long before this the very circumstances of common worship can do much to mortify fastidiousness and religious self-regard.

Moreover, the Church is not a collection of prize specimens, but a flock. Though we cannot return to the family action of the primitive community, the corporate and co-operative ideal must always remain true for Christianity; and has always controlled the Church's choice of liturgical forms. So in the Apocalyptic vision, the worship is genuinely congregational: an opportunity for the whole Body, sinking differences of understanding and feeling, to join Angels and Archangels, saints and elders, and all the creatures of the earth and sea in praising and glorifying the Holy Name. The *Sanctus* is the prayer of prayers for Christians, and the essential preliminary of Holy Communion, because it is thus world-embracing as well as world-transcending, and enfolds all levels and kinds of worship in one adoring act. The primitive conception of liturgical worship, as Dr. Frere has pointed out, was that of a concerted act of adoration in which everyone, from Bishop to neophyte, should have something to do, in word, gesture, movement, chant, or service; though not of course necessarily the same thing. But such joint action is impossible without an agreed pattern, a liturgy; even though this pattern be of the simplest kind.

— *Worship*

THE COMMUNION:
THIS SIGN WHICH DOES WHAT IT DECLARES

We come to the last, completing action in the mystery of the Eucharist; the communion of the faithful with each other and with Christ. Here it is that the experience of the Church rises to its height; and in consequence this action has seemed to many groups of Christians so central in its wonder and significance, that it has overshadowed all other aspects of the Liturgy and even displaced its ancient name.* The soul's approach in penitence and supplication, that oblation of life under tokens which is the very heart of man's worship, even the adoring gratitude with which he welcomes the coming of the Holy to bless and consecrate the gifts — all, in fact, that represents the union of the Praying Church with the eternal self-offering of Christ — is brushed aside or given a merely preparatory value. The whole meaning and aim of the liturgic drama is found in giving and receiving of the Bread of Life. Eucharist, with its emphasis on the adoration of God, vanishes. Communion, with its emphasis on man's need, takes its place....

Thus that communion of the faithful which is indeed the climax of the Liturgy should never be detached from the total Eucharistic moment of which it is a part. Its deepest, most sacred meaning is only understood by us when we perceive it to be the inevitable culmination of a close-knit act of sacrificial worship; an act which can never be that of individual fervor, but always that of the whole Christian family, transcending yet including in itself the separate movements and longings of each of its members. How completely the liturgic pattern here rebukes those who come to religion for the sake of their own souls; and, valuing its sacraments as means to the satisfaction of their own spiritual needs, ignore both their corporate responsibility in respect of the

---

*Editor's note: Underhill means here that in many Anglican churches the Eucharist is described as "Holy Communion."

whole Eucharistic action, and the place of that whole action in the vast economy of God.

For here the small self-offering of man in his wholeness is met by the Divine generosity, and transformed to His supernatural purpose; and the separate experiences of individual devotion are to be esteemed only as fragments of this one sublime experience of the Bride of Christ.

•

Thus it is only when costly and humble adoration, lost in the tide of worship and bowed down before that which it can never understand, has reached its height, that the soul can draw near to receive the food of Eternal Life. Then, the joy of giving is met and completed by the joy of welcoming love. By a series of profound contemplations, expressed in dramatic action and disclosing each aspect of her relation to God, the Church has moved towards communion with Him. So, too, in so far as the individual life is concerned, it is only those who have accepted the long, exacting discipline of preparation, who have offered themselves in oblation, given themselves to intercession, and finally surrendered all to the triune consecrating Power, who can enter into the depth and fullness of that mysterious communion in which man feeds upon the self-given Divine life.

Communion, then, must ever be thought of as the completion, the fruit of sacrifice; having, indeed, no meaning or reality without sacrifice. We spread out in time the successive phases of our Eucharistic worship and celebrate them one by one, because we live in time, and are bound to succession. But in those depths of the soul where Eternity is present, all are brought forth simultaneously as part of the single creative action of God; transforming and reconciling the world and each soul in the world to Himself by the besetting action of His Spirit, and making each soul a partaker of the divine nature....

Here, in the wide and generous distribution of the spiritual food to all, and in the intensity of love which is bent upon each, the utmost needs of corporate and personal religion are met and reconciled.

Christians hardly think enough of this aspect of their faith; the stooping-down of the Divine splendor and charity, not once but all the time, to save, transfigure, and complete all life. "Give me thy love and thy grace, for that is enough for me!" said St. Ignatius; offering his limited freedom, and asking in return that the very life of the Godhead might enter and endow his little soul. The disproportion is startling; yet the humblest communicant, who can give no more, receives no less. Going up to the altar he reaches out through Christ to the Eternal Reality of God, and shares the central experience of the saints. Here the Shekinah, the abiding glory and power of the Lord pressing in upon life, which is the true theme of Biblical history, is present; and the prayer of approach can only be "Lord, I am not worthy! nevertheless behold thy slave — be it unto me according to thy Word! ... "

•

Two movements merge in the real act of communion. First, the creature's profound sense of need, of incompleteness; its steadfast desire. "Blessed are they who hunger and thirst after righteousness," who crave for God, for the Holy and Eternal, and set their longing upon Him for Himself alone; sanctifying that emotional life which is the driving force of the will.... Next a humble and loving acceptance of God's answer to that prayer of desire, however startling, disappointing, unappetizing it may be; bread that seems hard, stale, and tasteless, the wine of eternity given in a common or ugly cup. It is not only at the visible altar or under the sacred traditional symbols that the soul receives the "rich bread of Christ." God, who comes to each in the "sacrament of the present moment," gives also in that sacrament the sustaining energy by which the present moment can be faced.

Therefore that which the Church does here, each repeated presentation of the theme of creation under liturgic forms, must be done again by each of her members hour by hour, in and with the homely stuff of circumstance. All must be given again and again;

not only at the visible altar, but at the invisible altar, on which man is to lay the oblation of his love and will, that it may be hallowed and made the medium of new life.

Here, by and in every event and experience, the poor soul and the rich God meet, and their mysterious and life-giving communion does or can take place. Here must be brought every pain and joy, desire and effort, accomplishment and frustration; to be met and divinized by the Divine self-giving life and love.

So here the Church, the Mother of Souls, looking towards Calvary, takes the ancient tokens of sacrifice and lifts them up to Eternity in the name of Christ her high priest, and with them satisfies her children's hunger and thirst. By this unceasing giving and receiving the whole of life is to be eucharisticized; this is the Christian task....

•

To live within the liturgy is to realize something of the heights and depths of Christian theism; its splendor, which confounds the soul even in attracting it, yet the simplicity and intimacy of those acts through which its most sacred gifts are made....

Yet if we were content to leave the matter thus, we should miss the Christian paradox; the fact that without man's small offering, nothing would have been done. The loaves must be given, and at his own cost, before they can become the gathering-points of the supernatural care, blessed, broken, and distributed, and so the Bread of Life given to the soul. "Why, that's a bit of my own baking!" said the woman in the old story, when the Holy Food was put into her hand. True, there is no proportion between the little human offering and the divine gift. Yet even here, where more than anywhere we feel our entire dependence and helplessness, will and grace rise and fall together, the double action between God and the soul is maintained....

•

The true Parousia comes not with observation, but bit by bit; through and in the ceaseless give and take between the living creature and that Life by which it lives. For we are maintained in a constant dependence on our environment, which is the very condition of our freedom; as we depend for life and growth upon that food which nourishes and the air that bathes our bodies, so on the grace that bathes and feeds our souls. . . .

So again and again, by this Drama that is more than a drama, and this Sign which does what it declares, the soul which has given itself is fed and maintained in the new status to which its self-surrender was the door. Here the life that was lost becomes the means of a new and increasing life found; a life indeed without limit, because it is no longer ours but the Absolute Life of God.   — *The Mystery of Sacrifice*

6

Practical Advice
From the Letters of Evelyn Underhill

Evelyn Underhill offered spiritual direction to a large number of individuals. Some of her letters demonstrate ways that she helped others to deal with the challenges of spiritual life. Her practicality, charm, and lack of stuffiness are evident in the letters that follow.

MAKE THIS LOVE ACTIVE

January 16, 1908

I feel a horrid diffidence in advising you on your last letter: it seems very presumptuous to do so — because, in a way, you have enough of your own to go on, and I, in advising you, can only go on my own experience, which may not be a bit of use to you. So, I shall probably make mistakes, and you must exercise your own judgment in accepting what I say. We are both in a very confusing forest, and the fact that I say I think I have found a path in one direction is no valid reason for you to alter your course.

Now, first, you have, you know, the "root of the matter" — and as long as you cling to that, you *can't* go far wrong. As your favorite St. Augustine said, "Love and do what you like!" If you like wrong things, you will soon find the quality of your love affected. This same condition of love governs everything else (e.g., it rules out, once for all, the idea of cash payments. Whether they are in force or whether they are not, the true lover, whether on the earthly or heavenly plane, has no thoughts to waste on them). It seems to me that your immediate job must be to make this love active and operative right through your life — to live in the light of it all the while, and act by it all the while — to make it light up your relations with other people; with nature, with life, with your work, just as much as it lights up immediate communion with Our Lord. Try to see people by His light. *Then* they become "real." Nothing helps one so much as that. Prayerful and direct intercourse is only half one's job; the other half is to love everything for and in God. This is of course only a longwinded way of saying that one has got to let faith issue in charity. When you have learnt to live within the love of God in this human and healthy sense, the question of sin will cease to be such a bogy as it is at present. Your attitude towards sin is really almost Calvinistic!! *Don't* dwell on it! Turn your back on it. Every minute you are thinking of evil, you might have been thinking of good instead. Refuse to pander to a morbid interest in your own misdeeds. Pick yourself up, be sorry, shake yourself, and go on again. Of course, it is deplorable that we should all hesitate to make temporal sacrifices for eternal gains — Thomas à Kempis is very bitter on the subject if you remember — but look back on the time when this aspect of the subject would not even have occurred to you, and ask yourself if your present unrest does not indicate progress? So with sins — as we advance, our conscience gets more delicate, and acts of self-help which once seemed almost laudable, now look hideous. Of course, because you had a "good time" before Christmas, and enjoyed devotion, you are now having a reaction and a flat time. But sticking to it in the flat times is of far more value both as service and as discipline — than luxuriating in religious emotion. It is what strengthens your spiritual muscles. Even the best people — even the saints — have always had to bear it: sometimes for years. It is a natural condition in the spiritual life. I know it is perfectly horrid when it happens — and I do *not* mean to be unsympathetic! But you must get enough grip to go on trusting in the dark. All the prayer in the world will not get you into a state in which you will always have nice times. You must not get slack: you must make a rule of life and go on with it steadily.

Now about meditation. Perhaps it may not be your "line." It is entirely a matter of temperament I believe. Some people cannot do it at all. Personally I can do it to a certain stage: but I know others who, with less practice, can pass easily and naturally into far deeper stages. In spite of all the mystics have told us, we are in it working with almost an unknown tool. Try to get rid of the visual image. Do you remember St. Teresa said of one of her nuns, "Sister X . . . has so *little* imagination that she always sees an image of the thing on which she meditates."

Try this way.

1. Put yourself into some position so easy and natural to you that you don't notice your body: and shut your eyes.

2. Represent to your mind, some phrase, truth, dogma, event — e.g., a phrase of the Paternoster or *Anima Christi,* the Passion, the Nativity are the sort of things I use. Something that occurs naturally. Now, don't think about it, but keep it before you, turning it over as it were, as you might finger some precious possession.

3. Deliberately, and by an act of will, shut yourself off from your senses. Don't attend to touch or hearing: till the external world seems unreal and far away. Still holding on to your idea, turn your attention *inwards* (this is what Ruysbroeck means by introversion) and allow yourself to sink, as it were, downwards and downwards, into the profound silence and peace which is the essence of the meditative state. More you cannot do for yourself: if you get further, you will do so automatically as a consequence of the above practice. It is the "shutting off of the senses" and what Boehme calls the "stopping the wheel of the imagination and ceasing from self-thinking" that is hard at first. Anyhow, do not try these things when you are tired — it is useless: and do not give up the form of prayer that comes naturally to you: and do not be disheartened if it seems at first a barren and profitless

performance. It is quite possible to obtain spiritual nourishment without being consciously aware of it!

Read *Holy Wisdom* by the Ven. Augustine Baker.

P.S. The dear cat sends his love; he was much flattered, as he perceives you to be a lady who understands cat-nature! His name is Jacob, because he supplants all other cats in the affections of those who know him — or so he thinks!   *— Letters*

DAILY ACTS, EXTERNAL INTERESTS

February 7, 1923

But you MUST settle down and quiet yourself. Your present state if encouraged will be in the end as bad for you spiritually as physically. I know it is not easy to do. Nevertheless it will in the nature of things come about gradually and I want you to help it all you know. If you allow rapture or vehemence to have its way too much, you risk a violent reaction to dryness, whereas if you act prudently you will keep the deep steady permanent peace, in the long run more precious and more fruitful than the dazzling light. But you won't do it by direct struggle — did you ever quiet a baby, or your dog, or any other excited bit of life, by direct struggle? You will do it, please, by steadily, gradually, and quietly turning your thoughts and prayers not so much to the overwhelming joy and wonder, as to the deep steadfastness of God, get gently accustomed to it, at home with it, *rest* in it. Let your night prayers be rather short, very quiet, more or less on a set form, not too "mental" and in the line of feeling of Psalm 23. Let yourself sink down into God's Love in complete dependence, and even though the light does seem to rush in on you, keep as it were the eyes of your soul shut, intent on falling asleep in Him. . . . During the day, doing your work, etc., it is I know very hard not to be distracted and absorbed. But remember you have no more right to be extravagant over this than over any other pleasure or craving. It is true you can and probably will find a balance in which you will live in a quiet spirit of prayer, able at all leisure moments —

and in the middle of your work — to turn simply and gently to God. But this will come only when all vehemence is eliminated.

Consider the sequence of daily acts, and your external interests as part of your service, part of God's order for you, and as having a proper claim on your undivided attention.

Take *special* pains now to keep up fully or develop some definite non-religious interest, e.g., your music. Work at it, consider it an obligation to do so. It is most necessary to your spiritual health; and you will very soon find that it has a steadying effect. "Good works" won't do — it must be something you really like for its own sake. (When this prescription was given to me by the wisest of saints, I objected strongly, but lived to bless him for his insistence! Now I hand it on to you.)

Otherwise, just for the present, do go as quietly as you can, about your work, etc., I mean. Avoid strain. If you could take a few days off and keep quite quiet it would be good, but if this is impossible at any rate go along gently, look after your body, don't saturate yourself the whole time with mystical books. I know you do feel tremendously stimulated all round; but remember the "young presumptuous disciples" in the *Cloud* [*of Unknowing*]! Hot milk and a thoroughly foolish novel are better things for you to go to bed on just now than St. Teresa.

Remember as a general rule, running right through the spiritual life, that the more any particular aspect or exercise attracts you, the more ordered, regular, moderate should be your use of it.

Don't have any lurking fear that you will lose the light by this kind of discipline — just the opposite, you will steady and tend to retain it.   — *Letters*

ACCEPT THE TIRESOME STUFF

Septuagesima, 1936

Don't think about being good! If you accept the very tiresome stuff the Lord is handing out to you, that's all He wants at the moment. "Let not your heart be troubled" if you can help it, is the best N.T. bit for the moment I think; but the more bovine or merely acquiescent you are the better. I know this will strike you as thin advice, but it is all I can give. Drop religion for the time being and just be quiet and wait a bit and God will reveal Himself again, more richly and closely than ever before.

— Letters

SEEING IN THE DARK

Advent Sunday, 1936

My love and blessing for your Retreat. I hope and believe it will be a time of peace for you and, if you will avoid all strain and let your soul slowly become tranquilized, you will begin, like the cats, to see a bit in the dark.

I do see that you must be constantly tempted to escape the pain of darkness by losing yourself in activity but I am not at all sure that it is a good thing to do. Physical exhaustion then reacts on your spirit and so we get a vicious circle! Do let this time be an entire withdrawal from work, the world, people, and the rest; an abiding in the emptiness where God alone is. I will be thinking of you much and shall expect you on the 6th anyhow, whether in the Pink or in the Drab and whatever the angle at which you are carrying the tail.   *— Letters*

THE DISCIPLINED LIFE

Lammas Day, 1937

I am sure the disciplined life based on the Sermon on the Mount is not easy! After all, it was never intended to be, was it? If you can get an hour a day (as much as possible consecutive and in the morning) you ought I think to be able to handle the situation even though just now the "sacrament of the present moment" may take rather a knobbly sort of form. Still God is in it and it is there that you have to find a way of responding to Him and receiving Him and are actually being fed by Him. Christianity does mean getting down to actual ordinary life as the medium of the Incarnation, doesn't it, and our lessons in that get sterner, not more elegant as time goes on?

As to deliberate mortifications — I take it you do feel satisfied that you accept *fully* those God sends. That being so, you might perhaps do one or two little things, as acts of love, and also as discipline? I suggest by preference the mortification of the Tongue — as being very tiresome and quite harmless to the health. Careful guard on all amusing criticisms of others, on all complaints however casual and trivial; deliberately refraining sometimes (*not* always!) from saying the entertaining thing. This does not mean you are to be dull or correct! but to ration this side of your life. I doubt whether things like sitting on the least comfortable chair, etc., affect you enough to be worth bothering about! But I'm sure custody of the Tongue (on the lines suggested) could give you quite a bit of trouble and be a salutary bit of discipline, a sort of verbal hair-shirt. I think God does provide quite a reasonable amount of material for self-denial, etc., in your life. This extra bit is for love. — *Letters*

STEADY, DOCILE PRACTICE

September 22, 1937

I feel the regular, steady, docile practice of corporate worship is of the utmost importance for the building-up of your spiritual life: more important, really, than the reading of advanced books like De Caussade [*Abandonment to Divine Providence*], though I am delighted that he attracts and helps you and feeds your soul. But no amount of solitary reading makes up for humble immersion in the life and worship of the Church. In fact the books are only addressed to those who are taking part in that life. The corporate and personal together make up the Christian ideal. You will find the "new attitude" you speak of — the simplicity, trust, and dependence — can be kept up, and that your Communions will play a very important part here, giving support of a kind you can hardly get in any other way, reminding you too of the great life of the Church, engulfing your little life, and, checking any tendency to individualism.   — *Letters*

DEALING WITH DRY TIMES

December 4, 1937

I have read the letter, and the paper you enclosed carefully; and I think the upshot of it all is, that you are still far too much inclined to make *feeling* the test of religion. All that matters in religion is giving ourselves without reserve to God, and keeping our wills tending towards Him. This we can always do; but to *feel* devout, fervent, aware of His presence, etc., is beyond our control. Everyone goes through "dry" times such as you are experiencing. They are of great value as tests of our perseverance, and of the quality of our love; and certainly don't mean that anything is wrong. All lies in how we take them — with patience, or with restlessness. As to the experience you describe, thank God for it; but don't worry if you never again have it. Such things do happen to many people from time to time, and especially at the beginning of a new phase in the spiritual life, but in this life such "awareness" is never continuous and its absence certainly does not necessarily mean that we are stopping it by our own fault. Just be simple and natural with God, ask Him to do with you what He wills, avoid strain and fuss of all kinds, and be careful to keep in charity with all men, and you will have done what is in your power. You say in your letter "below everything, I believe I'm in a way very quiet and happy" — well, *that,* not the fluctuating surface moods, represents your true spiritual state, and is the work of God. Give Him thanks for it and trust it and don't bother about the variable weather.   — *Letters*

AN HOUR IN THE MORNING

April 12, 1939

I shall be only too delighted if I can be of any help about your prayers. But I am rather frightened of giving detailed advice to anyone I do not know personally: as every one differs in temperament, capacity, etc., their prayer must differ too. So please take anything I say with a grain of salt.

I think an hour in the morning is enough at present and should not be added to; so the question is, how to use it best. Without being too rigid, or watching the clock, try dividing it roughly into 3 periods of about 20 minutes each.

(a) Will be given to a short N.T. reading and a meditation based on it, leading to

(b) Prayer, including adoration, intercession, and a review in God's presence of the duties, etc., of the coming day, especially the contacts which may be difficult, or uncongenial jobs.

(c) Spiritual reading.

The point about this plan is that the meditation leads on naturally to prayer; and as soon as you perceive it has done this, you can drop it (because it has then done its work) and continue with that intercourse with God which it will have set going. And, on the other hand, if it is a "bad day," the meditation gives you something definite to do and a subject to attend to and think about which will help to control wandering thoughts.

As to subject, there are lots of books which provide set subjects, points, etc. But I think myself the best and simplest way is just to take some point from one's daily N.T. reading, either the appointed Church lesson or whatever it may be, and, asking God for His light, to brood on it in His presence till it leads you into acts of penitence, love, worship, as the case may be.

No fixed rules can safely be laid down, because some people are more imaginative and others more logical in their ways of meditating, and each should follow their *attrait* and not try to force themselves into a particular method. Prayer should never be regarded as a science or reduced to a system that ruins it, because it is essentially a living and personal relationship, which tends to become more personal and also more simple, as one goes on.

Have you read *How to Pray* by J. N. Grou? I think that is one of the best short expositions of the essence of prayer which has ever been written; and of course there is much in his *Hidden Life of the Soul* too, which would be very useful to you.

On a much lower level, but still extremely good within its own limitations, is a small book called *How to Meditate,* published by S.P.C.K. in *Little Books on Religion* (2d.!); its directions are extremely clear, without being too rigid.

Beware of the elaborate arrangements of Preludes, Points, and so on which are set out in some devotional books; they only lead to unreality. And do not try to go on too long — ten minutes for the actual meditation will probably be enough at first. If there is anything else you want to know, please do not hesitate to write again, or else come in one day for a talk when you return to London.   — *Letters*

GO AT GOD'S PACE, NOT YOUR OWN

April 27, 1939

Thinking over our talk yesterday afternoon, I felt that perhaps it might be a help if I jotted down one or two points for you to consider at your leisure, without the worry of trying to remember just what was said! But if on the other hand you don't feel the need of this — then please ignore this letter.

(1) I am sure you ought to go very slowly and quietly — not only for the sake of your mind and body but still more for that of your soul. God in revealing Himself to you, put you at the beginning of a long road, and you must go at His pace, not your own (or mine!). "Tarry thou the Lord's leisure: be strong and He

shall comfort thy heart: and put thou thy trust in the Lord." That is a grand verse for you.

(2) Make up your mind from the first to ignore the ups and downs of the "spiritual climate." There will be for you as for everyone sunny and cloudy days, long periods of dullness and fog, and sometimes complete darkness, to bear. Accept this with courage as part of the Christian life. Your conversion means giving yourself to God, not having nice religious feelings. Many of the Saints never had "nice religious feelings"; but they did have a sturdy self-oblivious devotion to God alone. Remember old Samuel Rutherford: "There be some that say, Down crosses and up umbrellas...but I am persuaded that we must take heaven with the wind and rain in our face."

(3) Beware of fastidiousness! You are highly sensitive to beauty, and whatever branch of the Church you join there will be plenty of things that offend your taste, although they are religious meat and drink to less educated souls, who are also the children of God! Those dreadful Protestant hymns for instance! (The Roman ones if anything are worse — but I don't suppose you have ever heard such popular favorites as "Daily, Daily, Sing to Mary" or "Sweet Sacrament I Thee Adore"!) *You* interpreted the heavenly music as rather like the best plain-chant. But if God had given the same experience to the charwoman, and He is no respecter of persons, *she* would probably have been reminded of "Onward, Christian Soldiers" or "Abide with *me*." The Church must provide for all her children at every level of culture and this is a discipline which it is often hard for the educated to accept! It provides splendid training in charity and humility.

(4) I think you ought to have a very simple and unexacting rule for your devotional life; so as to get some order into it, but without worry and strain. Waking early as you do, I think you could at least spend 15 minutes with God either waiting silently on Him, praying or adoring, reviewing in His presence the duties, etc., of the coming day, or reading and brooding upon a psalm or a passage in Thomas à Kempis. Also in the last quarter- or half-hour of your afternoon rest, you could do this or read a

devotional book. I think you would gain by getting familiar with the psalms, making a list of those that help your prayer and using one at least each day. Psalms 25, 27, 42, 63, 51, 103, 116, 130, 139, 145, 148 for instance; 134 is a nice bed-time psalm!

Read a little of the New Testament every day.

(5) On the England or Rome question, *The Anglican Armoury* by H. Beevor gives that side, and *The Spirit of Catholicism* by Karl Adam, the best view of the Roman position but the author is considered very liberal! And more appreciated by Anglicans than R.C.s. In a book of mine called *Worship* I have a chapter on the Anglican position in which I have tried to state what seems to me the truth of the matter: and also some chapters on the Eucharist.

— *Letters*

BE SIMPLE AND DEPENDENT

May 3, 1941

People sometimes get St. John of the Cross by the tail! Self-occupation, including religious self-occupation, is always wrong, though often disguised as an angel of light.

This is the first thing I should say — Just plain self-forgetfulness is the greatest of graces. The true relation between the soul and God is the perfectly simple one of a childlike dependence. Well then, be simple and dependent, acknowledge once for all the plain fact that you have nothing of your own, offer your life to God and trust Him with the ins and outs of your soul as well as everything else! Cultivate a loving relation to Him in your daily life; don't be ferocious with yourself because that is treating badly a precious (if imperfect) thing which God has made.

As to detachment — what has to be cured is desiring and hanging on to things for their own sake and because you want them, instead of offering them with a light hand and using them as part of God's apparatus; people seem to tie themselves into knots over this and keep on asking themselves anxious questions on the subject — but again, the cure is more simplicity! They *must* shake themselves out of their scruples. The whole teaching of St. John of the Cross is directed to perfecting the soul in charity, so that all it does, has, says, is, is transfused by its love for God.

This is not a straining doctrine, though a stern one, as of course it does mean keeping all other interests in their place and aiming at God all the time.   — *Letters*

ANXIETY AND SUFFERING

Ascension Day, 1941

This intense craving for activity, freedom, doing work, is natural to you and me and hard to give up. But it is quite clear that it is something one must be prepared to give up if one is really to be "abandoned." And praying for people, however dryly and inadequately, may and often must be an exchange for instructing them! "Our Lord taught great perfection on the Cross" — doing nothing at all, but just accepting the situation and offering it to God.
                                                              — *Letters*

DO NOTHING AT ALL

October 15, 1939

I think from what you say, you are doing very well with your prayer. Everyone finds it difficult now, with all the distractions and anxieties that crowd on us. Nevertheless these are the circumstances in which we are now called to serve God; and the very best thing we can do to help the world's suffering is to lift it up to Him. Our own suffering and anxiety too can be dedicated and united to the Cross. Christ did not come to save us from trouble but to show us how to bear trouble.

Do you know this bit from Gerlac Petersen's *Fiery Soliloquy with God*? "Let every circumstance and event find thee standing firm like a square stone.... So much the more precious and glorious is virtue before Our Lord as agitated by contrary and diverse storms, occupations, tumults, and conflicts, it shall be found more constant; nor has it ever truly taken root in us, in time of rest and tranquillity, if it shall fail in time of tribulation.... For to him who bravely conquereth and not to him who avoideth the fight or dissembleth will be given the hidden manna and a new name." — *Letters*

7

Glory

Here is a final word about the radiance of God's life in us —
here and hereafter. In this selection Underhill writes with a cer-
tain passionate vocabulary, reaching to describe the beauty of our
life with God and the life to come. Let her lead you, deeply, into
the glory of God's presence.

Thine is the Kingdom, the Power, and the Glory. The prayer in
which is contained the whole movement of man's interior life,
the substance of his communion with God, is summed up in this
delighted declaration of the independent perfection, the unspeakable transcendence of the Holy. Before that reality, that majesty,
that energy, that splendor, his own needs, his own significance
vanish. Abba, Father. It is true that the infinite God is the Father
of my soul, that I have a certain kinship with the Abiding, a privilege of co-operation. Higher than my highest, He is yet nearer
than my inmost part. But in the last resort, I stand entranced and
abased before the majesty, the otherness of that Infinite God....
   Glory is the final word of religion, as joy is its final state. The
sparks and trickles of the Supernatural which come to us, the
hints received through beauty and through sacrifice, the mysterious visitations and pressures of grace reaching us through the
conflicts, rebellions, and torments of the natural world — all these
are earnests of a Perfection, a Wholeness yet unseen: as the small
range of sound and color revealed by the senses witness to the

unseen color and unheard music of a Reality which lies beyond their narrow span. All within the created order points beyond itself, to the uncreated Kingdom, Power, and Glory. No life, no intelligence reaches perfection; yet in each there is a promise of the Perfect. Each comes up to its limit, and in so doing testifies to that which lies beyond it; the unlimited splendor of the Abiding, the Glory of the living God. So too the creature's prayer comes up to its limit, and ends upon a word, a reality, which we can neither define nor apprehend.

All thy works praise thee, O Lord,
And thy saints give thanks unto thee.
They shew the glory of thy kingdom,
And talk of thy power:
That thy power, thy glory, and mightiness of thy kingdom
Might be known unto men. (Psalm 145:10–12)

Yet even this Kingdom, Power, and Glory, this threefold manifestation of the character of God, is not ultimate. The appeal of man's prayer is to a reality which is beyond manifestation. All these are Thine; but we reach out to Thee. Beyond the wall of contradiction, beyond the Light that is not God, almost imperceptible to the attentive creature and yet the ground of its being and goal of its prayer, is the secret Presence; the Thou in whom all things inhere, by whom all live. Behind every closed door which seems to shut experience from us He is standing; and within every experience which reaches us, however disconcerting, His unchanging presence is concealed. Not in the wind which sweeps over the face of existence to change it, not in the earthquake which makes sudden havoc of our ordered life, not in the overwhelming splendor and fury of the elemental fire: in none of these, but in the "voice of gentle stillness," speaking from within the agony and bewilderment of life, we recognize the presence of the Holy and the completing answer to the soul's completed prayer. We accept Thy Majesty, we rejoice in Thy Power and Thy Glory; but in Thine unchanging quiet is our trust. We look beyond the spiritual to Spirit, beyond the soul's country to the personal Origin and Father of its life.

"This is our Lord's will," says Julian of Norwich, "that our prayer and our trust be both alike large." Step by step we have ascended the hill of the Lord; and here at the summit of our beseeching, conscious of our own littleness and the surrounding mystery, we reach out in confidence to the All. The last phase of prayer carries the soul forward to an entire self-oblivion, an upward and outward glance of awestruck worship which is yet entinctured with an utter and childlike trust. Abba, Father. Thine is the kingdom, the power, and the glory. Thou art the Beginning and the End of the soul's life. — *Abba*

Sources

Abba: Meditations Based on the Lord's Prayer. London: Longmans, Green and Co., 1940. Copyright © 1981 by A. R. Mobray & Co., Ltd. Reproduced by permission of Morehouse Publishing, Harrisburg. Pennsylvania.

The House of the Soul, in *Concerning the Inner Life with the House of the Soul.* London: Religious Book Club, 1948. Reproduced with permission of the Estate of Evelyn Underhill.

The Letters of Evelyn Underhill. Edited by Charles Williams. Westminster, Md.: Christian Classics, 1989. Reproduced by permission of the Estate of Evelyn Underhill.

The Mystery of Sacrifice: A Meditation on the Liturgy. London: Longmans, Green and Co., 1938. Copyright © 1991 by Morehouse Publishing. Reproduced by permission of Pearson Education Limited.

Mysticism: A Study in the Nature and Development of Man's Spiritual Consciousness. New York: New American Library, 1955. Reproduced with permission of the Estate of Evelyn Underhill.

Mystics of the Church. Cambridge: James Clark and Co. Ltd., © 1925. Reproduced by permission of Morehouse Publishing, Harrisburg, Pennsylvania.

Practical Mysticism. New York: E. P. Dutton & Co., Inc., 1915. Copyright © 1991, reproduced by permission of Eagle Publishing.

The School of Charity: Meditations on the Christian Creed. Harrisburg, Pennsylvania: Morehouse Publishing, © 1991. Reproduced by permission of Pearson Education Limited.

The Spiritual Life. New York: Harper & Row [1937]. Copyright © 1937, 1938, 1955 by Hodder and Stoughton. Reproduced by permission of Morehouse Publishing, Harrisburg, Pennsylvania.

Worship. New York: Harper & Brothers, © 1937. Copyright © 1991, reproduced by permission of Eagle Publishing.

Original page references follow:

1. The Spiritual Life

What Is Mysticism? From *Practical Mysticism,* 1–6, 9–10

What Is the Spiritual Life? From *The Spiritual Life,* 15–17, 18–20, 20–21, 22–23, 23–25, 26–30, 30, 30–31, 31–32, 33–34, 34–35, 35–36, 36–37, 38–40

The Spiritual Life as Co-operation with God: From *The Spiritual Life,* 83–86, 87–90, 91–92, 92–93, 95–99, 102–4, 104–5, 107–9, 109–11, 113

2. The House of the Soul

(All Selections from *Concerning the Inner Life with the House of the Soul*)

The Soul's House: Not Too Big an Idea: From *The House of the Soul,* 65–66, 66–67, 67–68, 69–70, 71–72, 73

The Ground Floor: A Well-Ordered Natural Life: From *The House of the Soul,* 74, 77, 77, 78–79, 80, 81, 83, 84, 85, 86

Wise Furnishings: Temperance, Moderation, Fortitude: From *The House of the Soul,* 87–88, 81, 94, 101–2, 107–8, 108, 108–9

When Charity Enters: From *The House of the Soul,* 138, 140–42, 143–44, 144–45, 145–46, 147, 147–48, 148

3. Aspects of Mysticism

Mysticism in the Bible: St. Paul: From *Mystics of the Church,* 29–30, 31–32, 34, 35, 38, 38, 39, 42, 44–45, 47–49

Franciscan Mysticism: From *Mystics of the Church,* 90, 92–94, 95, 100, 101, 101–2, 103–4, 105, 107–8, 108–9

Some Protestant Mystics: From *Mystics of the Church,* 223, 223–24, 224–26, 226, 226, 226–27, 228–29, 230, 231, 232, 233, 233, 234, 234, 235, 235, 236, 236, 236–37

4. The Soul's Journey

The Characteristics of Mysticism: From *Mysticism,* 81, 81, 93, 93, 94

The Awakening of the Self: From *Mysticism,* 180–81, 196, 197, 197, 197

The Purification of the Self: From *Mysticism,* 201, 204, 204

Detachment: From *Mysticism,* 205, 208, 208, 216

The Illumination of the Self: From *Mysticism,* 258, 259, 264–65

Introversion: Contemplation: From *Mysticism,* 335, 335, 347–48, 348

The Dark Night of the Soul: From *Mysticism,* 395, 396

The Unitive Life: From *Mysticism,* 446, 447

Divine Fecundity: From *Mysticism,* 450

Glorified: From *The School of Charity,* 63–73

5. Worship

The Nature of Worship: From *Worship,* 3–10, 11–13, 13–16, 17–19

The Principles of Corporate Worship: From *Worship,* 83–84, 85–87, 88–89, 89–91, 91–94, 95, 96, 96–98, 98–99

The Communion: This Sign Which Does What It Declares: From *The Mystery of Sacrifice,* 58, 59–61, 61–62, 64–66, 66, 67–68, 69–70, 72

6. Practical Advice

7. Glory